Magical G

Exploring the Spi   ʌature
of Tre

Philip Heselton

Magical Guardians
Exploring the Spirit and Nature of Trees

©1998 Philip Heselton

ISBN 186163 057 3

Internal photographs by the author, apart from that on the dedication page which is be Kenneth Heselton and that on page 4 which is by Nick Howson
Internal illustrations by Lesley Wilkinson
Cover design by Paul Mason

Published by:

Capall Bann Publishing
Freshfields
Chieveley
Berks
RG20 8TF

DEDICATION

In memory of my mother
Joan Heselton
(13th November 1919 - 1st January 1998)
who first took me to the woods
and helped to open my eyes
to the spirit within.

By the same author:

Skyways and Landmarks Revisited
(with Jimmy Goddard and Paul Baines) [1985]
Earth Mysteries - An Exploratory Introduction
(with Brian Larkman) [1985]
Tony Wedd - New Age Pioneer [1986]
The Elements of Earth Mysteries [1991]
Secret Places of the Goddess [1995]
Earth Mysteries (Element Library Series) [1995]
Mirrors of Magic [1997]

Acknowledgements

This book has been in incubation for at least seven years, and I have been most encouraged by the continuing support of friends who persuaded me that the project was worthwhile.

Those who have helped and encouraged include Karen Atkin, Michael Barwell, Ian Bell, John Billingsley, Sheila Broun, Hilary Byers, Linda Carr, Amanda Class, Kiri Clay-Egerton, Kim and Tracey Dent-Brown, Jane and Bob Dickinson, Audrey Dunne, Robin Ellis, Ben Fernee, Chris Fletcher, Jimmy Goddard, Timothy Good, Brian Green, James Hamilton, Jerry Hardman-Jones, Jeremy Harte, Aidan Heselton, Kenneth Heselton, Owen Heselton, Penny Hill, Nick and Hilary Howson, Louise Jennings, Jayne Jones, Mary Long, John Merron, Marian Mozley, Jonathan Mullard, Brian Richardson, Jill Smith, Ian Taylor, Marion Toffolo, Bob Trubshaw, Julie Venner, Kay Watkins, Samantha White, Herbert Whone, Derrick and Anthea Wilbie-Chalk and Lesley Wilkinson.

I would particularly like to thank Lesley Wilkinson for the drawings which illustrate Chapter 6. These provide a striking contrast to the photographs which illustrate the rest of the book; Kiri Clay-Egerton for particular encouragement and permission to quote from an unpublished manuscript on trees; and Robin Ellis for his support and for permission to quote at length from his article "*The Woods Between the Worlds*".

And, of course, I must thank all those writers whom I quote, whose insights and expressive prose I value greatly.

But I must, above all, thank the trees themselves, who have given freely of their essence, and the wild woods, who have given me inspiration, courage and the beginnings of wisdom.

Contents

About the Artist

Lesley Eleanor Wilkinson holds a B.A. Honours in Fine Art. She has worked as a free-lance artist for a number of years producing artwork for Ebony, Lambs to the Slaughter and Peninsular Record Companies and illustrations for a variety of small press magazines. Ian Spence's book *The Sekhmet Hypothesis* (Bast Publications) is the only other full length book to feature her illustrations. In addition to being an artist she is also writer, editor and shaman/priestess. She is currently working on a variety of artistic and literary projects and becoming increasingly involved in theatre and dance.

Foreword

There is at the present time an unprecedented interest in trees which, at its roots, is both ecological and personal in motivation, for it combines our relationship with the Earth with an awareness of the innermost parts of our being. There is also a growing recognition of the importance of trees for the wellbeing of our planet, and campaigns to save trees, whether in the Amazon rain forests, on the North American watersheds or in suburban streets, have their origins in this awareness.

And yet, trees are more to us than this. Most people will admit to loving trees and acknowledge some special affinity with them. Parks, woods and forests have always popular destinations for recreational pleasures, and amenity tree-planting has never been so widespread. Yet at the same time, there is often an irrational fear of trees.

This book explores the reasons we feel as we do about trees, looking at the truth of what lies just below the surface - that trees have spirit as we do and that we can communicate with them in certain circumstances. It also shows that each tree has its own distinctive character and personality and that this explains much of the folklore and legends which have become attached to them.

Trees are not just isolated individuals - they live in community and in relationship to the land, as we do ourselves. In this book we explore that relationship and ways we can benefit from contact with trees, looking particularly at inspiration and healing.

1

Essentially, whilst we have duties to trees as their co-inhabitants of the Earth, it is perhaps more fruitful to look at them as our guardians, who have been on Earth much longer than we have and who, as individuals, live much longer than us. There is wisdom and knowledge there and it is in our own interests, as well as those of the planet, that these sources of wisdom are respected, listened to and heeded.

Chapter 1

Living With Trees

"I do not need to dwell on the symbolism of a tree; it has been part of the song and legend of every human society."
                                                    Boutros Boutros-Ghali

This is a book with a difference, a book which acknowledges trees as a group of wise beings with whom we share the Earth, and from whom we can learn if we approach them in the right way.

It is not primarily a botanical book, or even an ecological one: it is a book based on experience - on how people perceive trees.

If I were to write a book about Portugal, for example, you might reasonably expect me to have at least visited that country on several occasions, to have met and conversed with its inhabitants and to have at least made a serious attempt to learn Portuguese.

And so it is with trees. Trees are people, if looked at in their own terms, and we need to talk with them if we want to build up any kind of relationship. In writing this book I wanted to find the universal essence behind trees, but didn't really know how to start until I realised that, to make any real progress, I had to learn from the trees themselves.

I call myself a pagan. This is not necessarily intended to indicate membership of some obscure, esoteric and secretive religious cult, but to show a certain attitude to life - a respect for nature and for the spirit which lies within all beings. In common with most, if not all, pagans, some of my earliest and most formative experiences have been linked with trees and woods.

Whenever I visited somewhere new, perhaps on holiday or having a picnic in the countryside, I always felt the strong desire to go off on my own to find my own special place. This was the theme of my book *"Secret Places of the Goddess"*[50] and, looking back on it, I can see now that, almost without exception, those places had trees - and usually one special tree - as a central element.

It is difficult to describe what I felt in such places, but there was certainly what I would now describe as a change in consciousness. Firstly, I could relax as the concerns of the everyday world faded away. My imagination - thoughts, ideas, possibilities - opened up like a flower emerging from the night. The trees were always comforting, but this was often accompanied by an excitement - the feeling that possibilities might actually become reality. Above all, there was a sense of rightness - that this is where I should be and this is what I should be doing. The trees taught me the meaning of what has been called "right livelihood" - doing what only I can do and being what only I can be. So I was strengthened and encouraged by the trees and, though I speak of it in the past tense, I still find comfort and support amongst them.

Certain trees have special meaning for me. The start of my involvement in what later came to be known as "Earth Mysteries" was symbolised by the Scots pine, and the excitement which it engendered. And beeches have been a great comfort to me. Beech groves on the tops of rolling hills have exuded a soothing balm in my times of depression and disturbance. Walking into such a grove, with the fallen leaves

5

and nuts and tree roots beneath my feet, feeling their grey-green bark with my hands and climbing their branches with my eye-beams, their presence has calmed and strengthened me and replaced anxiety with joy, which always lasts way beyond the original experience.

Much later in my life, I came home to the ancient Craft which had been my faith in earlier lives, and realised again the significance to me of the hawthorn - the witch's tree.

Others, far more poetically-inclined than myself, have had similar experiences, from the story-tellers of old to the poets and writers of more recent years and my own friends who have revealed deep and very personal encounters with trees. These are really the heart of this book - accounts of ways in which people have met and communicated with trees on their own terms and have gained in wisdom as a result.

We all know a tree when we see one, even if we can't define it botanically. And trees are special to most of us, though we might find it difficult to pin down the cause. Here, Kim Taplin helps us and provides some clues to our attraction:

> "Because they are primeval, because they outlive us, because they are fixed, trees seem to emanate a sense of permanence. And though rooted in earth, they seem to touch the sky. For these reasons it is natural to feel we might learn wisdom from them, to haunt about them with the idea that if we could only read their silent riddle rightly we should learn some secret vital to our own lives; or even, more specifically, some secret vital to our real, our lasting and spiritual existence."[107]

In this book, I explore these themes further and help to explain some of our fascination with trees.

England is one of the least wooded countries in Europe. Yet, even in the hearts of our big cities we are rarely out of sight of a tree. Even children who have never seen a sheep or a horse are familiar with trees and they form a subject for artistic expression from an early age. In other words, trees are a familiar part of our life. We may well have taken them for granted and not really looked at them, but they are something to which we can relate: they are not alien.

We notice trees because they are big. Even the slowest-growing ones quickly outstrip us in height, and trees have been planted for hundreds of years because of the visual impact which their size makes on town square and country park alike.

On Having Roots

Trees stay in one place and, once we begin to notice them at all, we incorporate them into the 'mental map' which we all make of our surroundings. Depending on their position, individual trees, clumps and woodland can be prominent features in the landscape in a way in which people and animals can never be because they move.

Most of us have the ability to move freely, yet we all have our habitual places - places where we like to sit still and let the world go by. Sometimes these places are quite specific. I remember a few years ago frequenting a pub on the riverside at Shrewsbury. While standing at the bar waiting for my pint of beer to be pulled, I noticed a framed portrait on the wall opposite, of a gentleman with quite distinctive features. My eyes then fell a little to notice unmistakably the man himself sitting on a chair immediately below. It was obviously his habitual seat and the portrait had been hung there in his honour.

In similar vein, my friend the late Fred Fletcher used to tell the story of the time when he was on holiday in an unfamiliar part of the country. He was a Quaker and had found the

8

location of the local Friends' Meeting House. On the Sunday he attended the morning Meeting for Worship. He was a little early and there was no-one else there, but since in Quaker tradition the meeting starts the moment the first worshipper takes their seat, he sat down in silent contemplation.

A few moments later, another individual walked in, obviously a member of the meeting who had been attending regularly for many years. The room was deserted apart from Fred, but the old man walked straight up to him and, in a clear voice, said "Friend, thou art sitting in my seat". Again, the specific place which was not to be altered by the mere presence of a newcomer!

Perhaps we all have this to some extent, and we may think of buses, cafes, doctor's surgeries or classes that we attend where we habitually sit in the same place, though perhaps not with the determination of Fred's old Quaker.

Indeed, these are the exceptions - the extreme end of the spectrum. Generally we are so busy that we make little direct impact on the landscape, like the early photographs of city streets which appeared deserted because the moving pedestrians were too fast to be captured on the slow photographic film in use at that time.

The Wisðom of Age

Part of the significance which trees have for us is their longevity: they live longer than we do, in most cases much longer. Even a relatively short-lived tree like the birch can make 80 years, oaks can live several hundred, and yews several thousand years, if not attaining literal immortality, as we shall see.

Trees can thus be seen as permanent features of our lives, growing imperceptibly throughout our "seven ages", acting as a steady reference point, a familiar and cherished background in front of which the drama of our life is played.

It is perhaps a direct consequence of their longevity that trees have a much slower pace of life than we do. We need to become more "rooted", at least for a time, in order to attune to their rhythms, as we shall see in Chapter 5.

Another consequence of their longevity, in terms both of species and of individuals, is that they have acquired qualities that can usually only be acquired over time - wisdom and knowledge. If it seems strange to attribute what may generally be thought of as human qualities to trees, read on ... for there is a fascinating story to unfold.

Life in Death and the Dissolution of Boundaries

The actual moment of death for a human being is usually fairly sudden and definite - one minute we are alive and the next minute we are dead. We may be ill beforehand, and there are certainly cases where people have been brought back from the dead - the so-called near-death experience - but the actual moment of death itself is both clear and quick.

Death is totally different for a tree. They do not die suddenly as we do. Indeed, oaks were traditionally said to be:

> "*Three hundred years growing*
> *Three hundred years living*
> *Three hundred years dying*"

Indeed, the technique of the oak, and possibly other trees, of becoming hollow in the middle is clearly a natural process which actually makes it more resistant to high winds, as the oaks in Windsor Great Park which withstood the 1987 hurricane ably demonstrated.

Death, for a tree, usually happens slowly and, even when a tree looks completely dead, life can spring up again, as Rupert Sheldrake recalls:

> *"My most vivid image of the rebirth of nature came to me when I was staying at the old family farmhouse in Farndon, a village on the River Trent near my home town, Newark. I was about four or five years old. Near the house, I saw a row of willow trees with rusty wire hanging from them. I wanted to know why it was there, and asked my uncle, who was nearby. He explained that this had once been a fence made with willow stakes, but the stakes had come to life and turned into trees. I was filled with awe."*[104]

This reminds me of the images of wands contained in the Rider/Waite tarot pack. These are not dead lumps of wood, but living branches with leaves sprouting forth. And there are many traditions of staffs being planted and then springing to life, such as Joseph of Arimathea's Glastonbury Thorn on Wearyall Hill and St. Etheldred's staff at Stow in Lincolnshire.

In trees, death can thus readily be seen as part of life. Indeed, for some trees, death may literally have no meaning, as Sir George Trevelyan explains of the yew:

> *"It is claimed that the great yew could be absolutely immortal. Grasp what it is doing. The central complex of bole and trunk often seems like a number of trees flowing into each other to make an entity of incredible strength. Then the branches around the central trunk dip down and reroot themselves so that, as a virtually new tree, they may send out further branches. Thus, theoretically at least, the process can go on till the ringed complex covers a great area."*[24]

Trees can thus demonstrate vividly the power of regeneration and the wheel of life, death and rebirth that is at the heart of the pagan religion. This is powerfully reflected in the annual cycle of new buds in the spring, opening out into the flourishing summer greenwood, the release of leaves in autumn to fall back to the earth, and the apparent death of the tree through winter until it is brought back to life the following spring. This is often a surprise and a wonder, as Elizabeth Goudge emphasises in *"The Herb of Grace"*:

"... on the lichened boughs of the old gnarled oak-trees the new coral-tipped young leaves were burning like candles. It was strange, thought Nadine, that creatures so gloriously fresh and young as those bright leaves could draw their life from anything so old and twisted as those oak-trees ... It gave one hope ..."[40]

Each tree is unique, and each one has its own character, if we can get to know it. Indeed, this character increases with age, as Richard Mabey observes:

"...Their shapes, their burrs and branch stumps and root-stocks are living records of what has happened to them historically. In their maturity trees are so etched with experience that they become recognizable not just as species but as individuals and then yet another kind of grain begins to develop - the accumulating layers of myth and affection that gather round ancient trees."[68]

The principle that the universe is ultimately, at its heart, one being, lies at the root of most ancient religions and philosophies. Whilst at least in our ordinary everyday lives we are happy in the illusion that we are separate and distinct beings, trees do not have these limitations and can merge into each other and into their environment at will - a living demonstration of that ancient principle. It is as if the slow growth of trees can achieve what is denied to rapid movement. In particular, if circumstances are right, trees, sometimes even of different species, can merge together into one being. They are teaching us, if we care to listen, that the artificial boundaries that we put up are not inevitable - they can be dissolved if we so desire, and we can experience the oneness of the universe.

Magical GuaRδians

The title of this book gives some idea of what I feel about our actual and potential relationship with trees. People and trees are equally part of the living being we call the Earth. However, whilst we have often used our powers unwisely and not in the best interests of the planet as a whole, trees have played a role which can be likened to a Mother or Guardian, as John Stewart Collis points out:

> "[Trees] hold up the mountains. They cushion the rain-storm. They discipline the rivers. They control the floods. They maintain the springs. They break the winds. They foster the birds."

It is this attitude to trees that I want to encourage. And in order to help do that, we need to be aware of the true nature of the community of trees and our historical and potential relationship with them.

Trees have physical uses and they also fulfill our spiritual needs. Indeed, these approaches are intertwined, and there is no clear division between them, as Kim Taplin points out:

> "Most of us make now too great a separation and distinction between the physical and the spiritual. On a walk in sun or rain we can still experience how shade and shelter were constantly added to the trees' other practical gifts to us when we lived closer to the earth. Then physical gratitude merged with the more numinous feelings. For there is a region where the two are

indistinguishable, where physical and spiritual health are one."

Stevenson evoked it in his Forest Notes (1876), when he wrote that:

' ... it is not so much for its beauty that the forest makes a claim upon men's hearts, as for that subtle something, that quality of the air, that emanation from the old trees, that so wonderfully changes and renews a weary spirit.'"[107]

We can, however, discern certain ways in which trees have been and continue to be useful to us in our everyday lives - as places, sources of materials and of physical comfort.

Trees as Meeting Places

Certain trees have taken up key positions in the landscape so that they give emphasis to a particular landform or the point at which a path moves out from one type of landscape to another, perhaps a watershed or the edge of a forest. They have therefore been remembered and become literally land-marks - marking the land and the paths that pass through it, and we shall see in Chapter 9 how people have recognised the significance of such trees and have followed nature in planting trees for themselves in significant locations and caring for them over generations.

Certain prominent and distinctive trees became talked about, perhaps as guides to those walking through unfamiliar country and, inevitably, became meeting-places for travellers. This led over time to several paths meeting at the one point, which became in turn a camp site and a moot (or meeting) point, where the community gathered to make decisions about matters affecting them.

An example local to where I grew up is Spelthorne in Middlesex. This is now just a public house at a crossing of two ancient roads, but it gave its name to the Hundred, an area within which justice was administered, and subsequently to a Parliamentary Constituency and a Local Authority. "Spel-" means speech, and so it was clearly originally marked by a thorn tree at the cross-roads where moots were held and decisions taken.

A few miles up the River Thames from Spelthorne lies Ankerwyke, where a large old yew tree survives, the only one of its size and age, according to Allen Meredith, in such a low-lying location. He is convinced that this was the actual spot on which the Magna Carta was signed, because of its age and historical associations, even in the 13th Century, rather than the usually favoured location of Runnymede, now on the opposite bank of the river.[24]

Trees can live on through place-names even after there is no physical evidence that they ever existed, and 'thorn', 'oak' and 'ash' and their variants are particularly common in certain areas. Trees have also been trysting-places for lovers and we are familiar with the carved initials, particularly on the smooth trunks of beech trees, from years gone by. There is that which is erotic about the tree, and the beech in particular, in the forms of its roots, trunk and branches which echo those of the human body, and it feels natural to embrace those whom we are with, leaning against the solid trunk, as it is that of the tree itself.

Indeed, Nigel Pennick tells us that:

> *"... marriages were solemnised beneath their branches in the tradition of the Elder Faith. After a Christian wedding in church, couples would go to a marriage oak to have their union blessed according to the customs of the Old Religion."*[92]

15

16

The eponymous closing chapter in Hardy's *"Under the Greenwood Tree"*, for example, is an evocative description of just such a celebration, with singing, dancing, feasting and drinking.

When the persecutions took hold, those who held to the Old Religion of witchcraft used to meet at night in the depths of the countryside under a great oak. And, whilst persecution has lessened so that they are no longer under fear of their lives, they still do so meet today, as much for the qualities inherent in the tree as with its remoteness.

Places of Refuge

Trees and caves are, in the popular imagination, the dwelling places of the most ancient of people. Remains have certainly been found in the relatively few caves that exist to bear this out, but there is no real way of knowing whether people actually lived in trees.

Perhaps the more important point, however, is that people can live in trees and have done so throughout recorded history, at any rate. The tree has certain qualities, particularly in summer, which enable someone sitting in its branches to see without being seen. This is a very powerful position to be in, with enemies threatening, because it is both a good look-out position and an effective hiding place. The oak in particular, because of the form of its branches and the thickness of its foliage, seems ideal for this purpose.

Indeed, the archetypal image of Robin Hood is of his band of outlaws using trees, and particularly the oaks of Sherwood Forest, if not to live in then certainly to move about, hide in when necessary and spy on whatever was happening on the ground.

And Charles II escaped his pursuers by hiding in the great oak at Boscobel, which act is commemorated in the numerous Bellarmine jugs which have the image of the king's face surrounded by oak leaves. They have been much sought after by adherents to the Old Religion because of the similarity which this image has to the Green Man, or foliate head of traditional carvings.

Trees have long been a refuge in both history and fiction. Initially, Defoe has Robinson Crusoe sleeping in a tree for fear of ravenous beasts:

> "... I went to the tree, and getting up into it, endeavoured to place myself so as that, if I should fall asleep, I might not fall; and having cut me a short stick, like a truncheon, for my defence, I took up my lodging; and having been excessively fatigued, I fell fast asleep, and slept as comfortably as, I believe, few could have done in my condition; and found myself the most refreshed with it that I think I ever was on such an occasion."[33]

Indeed, climbing trees seems to be a universal activity, particularly amongst children, perhaps because trees are fellow beings we can play with - and in! Certain trees, such as oak and beech, are, by their nature, more suitable for climbing than, say, birch, elder, hawthorn and hazel, although Robert Frost's poem "The Birch" links the nature of the tree in a striking manner with the problems associated with climbing it. Nevertheless, most have the potential for hiding in particularly those that form "impenetrable thickets".

The very darkness under the spreading branches of a tree has scope for hiding and seeing out without being seen, the circle of branches literally acting as a 'circle of invisibility'. Arthur Ransome uses this quality when he describes the place chosen by the Amazons to hide their boat:

"He had crawled right in under the branches of the oak till he could touch its huge trunk. On the other side its branches hung out over the river, the tips of them sweeping the water, and there, under these branches and tied to one of them, hidden so that it could hardly be seen from the river or from the shore except by someone who had crept in under the tree, was a long, narrow, native rowing boat."[97]

A natural development of climbing and hiding in trees is the construction of a tree-house. Nowadays we tend to think of them as being primarily for children's play, but tree-houses are a normal construction in many parts of the world such as New Guinea. There is also a deeper need for them, as John Ebdon has pointed out:

"Accessible only by a precarious retractable rope ladder it was to become my sanctuary from which, unseen, I could look down upon the world of grown-ups through its canopy of leaves ... The Great Oak became part of my life. On leave from the RAF in the dark days of the war, I would climb into my bower as I did as a child, temporarily know peace of mind, and briefly feel secure before returning to fight in the air again. To me, the tree spelt stability."[123]

Anthony Aikman[5] takes things still further back than the time when people were living in trees by referring to 'the nesting instinct' and then showing how trees have been used for dwellings, places of contemplation and entertainment from the earliest recorded history up to modern times.

Tree-houses have on occasions been quite elaborate and there is at least one, dating from the 18th Century, which is now listed as being of architectural or historic interest. Indeed, in Normandy there is an 800-year old church in an oak tree reminding us of the spiritual nature of our relationship with trees that we shall be exploring in this book. Photographs show this church as something almost organic, growing out of the tree itself rather than imposing rigid lines upon it.

Probably this is one of the elements of a truly satisfying tree-house for, unless one is there from dire necessity, one is presumably attracted by the qualities which the tree possesses and this leads on quite naturally to an 'organic' type of house, using and flowing with the forms of the branches.

My friend, Nick Howson, told me about a tree-house which his father constructed, although perhaps 'constructed' is not quite the right word. There was an old poplar at the bottom of his garden which he had pollarded. He then had the idea of building a platform about 5 feet across on the top of the remaining stump. The new shoots which always start to grow following pollarding grew round the platform and then up. He let them grow freely until they were tall enough to meet at the top, when he tied them together and encouraged them to intertwine. He kept an entrance to the platform free and pruned the shoots from inside to keep a clear space.

The shoots have now grown, in thickness as well as height, providing an organic-looking but effective tree-house, which has been enjoyed by children and others for many years.

Arbours and bowers are other places of refuge which, traditionally, have used and adapted the natural forms of trees and climbing plants. They have long been an integral part of the formal garden, often made by growing trees (particularly hornbeams) in a circle, leaving a small gap as an entrance, and then tying and grafting them together at the top when they had grown sufficiently tall to accommodate two people seated.[1] The essence of such places is that they were private and used for romantic or other purposes that required withdrawal from the outside world.

The Use of Wood

As well as living with trees, we also live off them. We cut them down, lop their branches, tap them for sap and resin, pick their fruits and nuts and gather their dead wood. This activity has continued for millennia and has often resulted in a ravaged landscape, largely denuded of tree cover, a process still continuing in many parts of the world. As Kim Taplin points out:

> "If we try to look at the matter as the oaks might look at it, we can see that trees represent an earlier indigenous population against which human beings have carried on a long, and in many parts of the world a now rapidly accelerating, campaign."[107]

Nevertheless, there is a harmonious way of living with trees, for they are living beings who produce wood, fruits and nuts, sap and resin. If we only take these products at a rate which allows regeneration, then our actions can be sustained indefinitely. This is living within our resources which, ultimately, is the only way to live.

The old ways of action, such as those of the native Americans, involve asking the trees before doing anything to them. The felling of a tree was only carried out after a long process which started by making sure that it was the right thing to do and that the timber was needed for a real purpose that could not be satisfied in a way that avoided the necessity for felling. Then the permission of the spirit of the tree was sought and, only when and if this had been obtained, were preparations made for the felling. Before this took place, they needed to make sure that the spirit of the tree had withdrawn before the axes were wielded.

All this implies an acknowledgement that we are dealing with spiritual beings who are worthy of respect but who may be willing to lay down their lives to help us.

One way in which the life of the tree is preserved is through the practice of coppicing. This involves controlling the growth of trees like willow and hazel by cutting back strongly every few years to allow new shoots to grow, which provide wood for a variety of purposes, where poles of various lengths and thicknesses are produced for fencing, furniture and all manner of items for everyday use. Such coppicing can be carried on indefinitely and is truly a form of regeneration. Some boles of hazel are thought to be over a thousand years old, and this is not unusual.

Whether or not people lived extensively in trees, they have certainly brought trees into their houses and used them in their construction. The simplest dwellings, similar to the tipi or yurt, were made from branches arranged in a cone shape tied together at the top. Indeed, well into the present century, charcoal-burners used such a construction for their huts when they needed to be on hand to tend their fires, as Arthur Ransome describes:

> *"At the edge of the wood, not far from the smoking mound, there was a hut shaped like a round tent, but made not of canvas but of larch poles set up on end and all sloping together so that the longer poles crossed each other at the top. On the side of it nearest to the mound there was a doorway covered with a hanging flap made of an old sack. ... Gradually their eyes grew accustomed to the darkness, and they saw that on each side of the hut a stout log divided off a place where there were rugs and blankets. Between the two logs there was an open space, where it looked as if there had been a small fire. The open light came through the doorhole. Not a speck of light came from between the poles of which the wigwam was made. Every chink had been well stuffed with moss. Overhead there hung a lantern, like their own camp lantern, from a hook at the end of a bit of wire. But it was not lit. High above them was pitch darkness, where the poles met each other at the pointed top of the hut."*[96]

Gradually buildings became more elaborate, sometimes using whole tree trunks, such as the 'cruck' cottages, using branches as they were for structural timbers, without much in the way of shaping. Even today, timber frame housing is common and is used particularly by those who are intent on building their own homes.

Wood-working has become one of the traditional skills in most parts of the world for making of a vast range of equipment to go inside our homes. The list is almost endless and includes furniture, cupboards and shelves, storage boxes, kitchen utensils, cradles and toys.

The wood of each type of tree has its own particular characteristics and came to be favoured for making specific items. Beech, for example, is prized for furniture whereas alder makes excellent charcoal, as well as underwater piles and foundations. Ash makes good poles and handles, whereas the flexible birch twigs are used for brooms. Willow is ideal for woven baskets and yew makes very elegant bowls and drinking vessels.

The Magic of Fire

If we can truly imagine ourselves into the place of the ancient people, we can see that fire is magical. Tony Wedd's account of how he felt that people first discovered how to make fire is worth recording. He says:

> "There are three candidates for our investigation: the spontaneous combustion of marsh gas in the ignis fatuus we call jackie lantern and will-o-the-wisp; the lightning flash setting fire to trees and dried undergrowth; and the accidental discovery of the firestick. The technical difficulty of the first is too high: to achieve results man had to learn by repetition, and this was too casual and chancy an affair to allow for any mistakes; which rules

out the second also, with the added difficulty that the scale of the fire would have been horrific: animals are frightened of flames, and it is our peculiarity that we overcame our fear and domesticated the phenomenon. We would have been unlikely to try our hand at a forest fire in the first place. We could only have begun with the firestick.

We are asked to believe that men accidentally discovered that you could spin a hard, dry stick in a hole or notch in another one, concentrating for a fairly arduous extension in time, until the two became flame-hot, and set fire to a pile of dried moss called tinder piled around the hole. Two items here are difficult to allow: the concentration, and the pile of tinder. But we can explain both if we accept the heightened sexuality hypothesis. Man was acting out the business of love-making when he rubbed his firestick so energetically in the hole. He brought to the symbolic mime the intensity he experienced in fucking; and he had piled the moss there to represent the female's pubic hair. In the ecstasy of an orgasm, the horror of the ensuing flames which any other animal would have felt was mitigated, even transmuted into excitement."[118]

Whilst grasses, certain types of fungus and even reindeer dung have been used for tinder, it is overwhelmingly until the last few hundred years wood that has been used to sustain that magical being that is not substance or quality but which warms, cooks and provides the environment for scrying.

This magical property of wood enhanced people's reverence for trees and their indwelling spirit. Fires became part of the seasonal festivals, such as the great hilltop Beltane and midsummer bonfires and the need fires between which cattle were passed. We still have bonfires on 5th November, originating not just in the Gunpowder Plot of 1605 but in the old festival of Samhain - the summer's end.

Nourishment and Healing

Fruits and nuts have been our foods since the time when we were gatherers, wandering from place to place with the seasons, knowing just the locations where trees would be found which would provide, not only fruit and nuts for food but sap and resin also, for it is likely that wines and incenses were some of the earliest preparations ever made.

Of course, our relationship with trees is far richer and more varied than the outline which I have given here. It encompasses the whole of what might be called the spiritual dimension to life and the way in which our own spiritual life is intertwined with that of the trees themselves. Trees are useful physically, but it is in the etheric and spiritual dimensions that we can relate to them most fruitfully, because they can teach us fundamental universal principles. This is revealed both in folklore and in the wealth of personal experiences which are the essential subject of this book.

Chapter 2

The Spiritual Life of Trees

"A tree says: A kernel is hidden in me, a spark, a thought, I am life from eternal life. The attempt and the risk that the eternal mother took with me is unique, unique the form and veins of my skin, unique the smallest play of leaves in my branches and the smallest scar on my bark. I was made to form and reveal the eternal in my smallest special detail."

Hermann Hesse - *Wandering*

As well as their practical uses, trees have made an important contribution to our spiritual life, by which I include artistic and literary inspiration as well as what has been classified as 'religious vision' or 'cosmic consciousness'. It would certainly also include such simple pleasures as enjoying a walk through the woods. The underlying thread linking these experiences is a contact with trees at a deeper level than everyday consciousness. This chapter looks under the surface and examines the spiritual life of trees.

Personal experience and the increasing wealth of written accounts has made it easier to accept what we might call "the hidden world". Instinctively, we seem to recognise that there is something beyond the physical form and that by changing our consciousness we can perceive other aspects or dimensions to what appear to be just everyday things. Although often

described in terms of "planes of existence", it is really a continuum, another dimension that we can, potentially, move into and around at will, not least because, whether we are aware of it or not, we also inhabit that dimension ourselves.

Explorers of these realms (which were well known in ancient times and written about in the myths and sagas) are piecing together the subtle geography and subtle anatomy, and guides have already been written to assist the traveller in those realms.

What seems to be emerging are five interlocking principles which it is important to grasp in order to gain a proper understanding of our relationship with trees. This is not the place to do more than summarise them, but much supporting evidence can be found in the works of such writers as James Lovelock[66], Rupert Sheldrake[103] and Fritjof Capra[18].

The Essential Unity

The first principle is one of the oldest and can be found in the teachings of most ancient philosophies and religions as well as in the findings of modern physics. It postulates that, at heart, the whole universe is one and that every part of it is at some level connected with every other part. Things appear in everyday life as separate, just as we, trapped in the illusion of what Alan Watts calls our 'skin-encapsulated ego', feel we are separate from everyone else. This separation is perfectly real when looked at in the ordinary way, but when seen from a different perspective, it dissolves into nothing. Ultimately, this is how psychic phenomena and divination work, because if we are all one then we can know the truth of everything directly.

The Dimensions of Life

Notwithstanding this, it is abundantly clear that in our ordinary everyday reality things are separate. But the very

mention of 'ordinary everyday reality' presupposes the existence of some other state of being with which it is being contrasted. Philosophies, religions and ways of being from the most primitive to present 'New Age' beliefs have affirmed that there are indeed other states of being. Whether we talk in terms of 'spiritual planes', 'levels' or 'vibrations' we are implying that there is more to existence than the normal everyday state and that by changing our consciousness we can become aware of other 'frequencies' that the universe operates on, of which, in normal circumstances, we are unaware. There is that part of us which survives physical death, for example, and can be reborn. When we become aware of that part we realise that it is in touch with a similar part in all other beings and from this can spring inspiration and deep knowledge.

The Subtle Body

Such awareness has been a constant theme in virtually all methods of healing and self-development from ancient times to the present day. Sensitives have recognised the existence of bodies more subtle than the physical and interweaving with each other. They have seen these subtle bodies as being composed of flows of energy, often extending outside the physical body and perceptible as the aura. Centres or vortexes of energy, known in Sanskrit as chakras, are also present, corresponding to the endocrine glands in the physical body.

One principle that seems established is that events and conditions manifest on the inner planes before they become apparent in the physical. Many diseases are of this nature and, with this awareness, not only can they be treated much sooner, but the underlying causes can be dealt with rather than just the physical symptoms.

The human body can thus be seen as a system of energies flowing into, out of and between the chakras, constantly

32

changing and, to the seeing eye, revealing conditions hidden to orthodox medicine.

Gaia and the Earth Spirit

Since the recognition of the science of ecology, it has become widely acknowledged that all of us who live on the Earth - people, animals, trees and other plants - are interconnected. Our lives are intimately intertwined and we know without doubt that what we do affects all the other beings with whom we share the Earth.

Following the work of James Lovelock[66], however, we can now go further and realise that the whole Earth is a living being in its own right - known to the ancient Greeks as the goddess Gaia - and that we, along with all other beings, are a part of her. This has profound implications for how we see ourselves and how we live, but for our present purposes its importance lies in our perception of the landscape for, if the Earth is indeed a living being, she too will have a subtle body, with an aura, chakras and energy flows operating within the landscape itself.

The Creation of Form

The work of Rupert Sheldrake[103] on what he calls 'morphogenesis' confirms much of the older teaching about the nature of the universe, and is highly relevant in our study of trees. He is a biologist who was not satisfied with the orthodox ways of explaining physical form in plants and animals. One of the unsolved problems in biology was the way in which the seed can contain the essence which eventually grows into the new member of the species. Sheldrake put forward the idea of the existence of some sort of mould or pattern which shapes the individual tree or animal of each species just as the field around a magnet can create a pattern in iron filings. He called this formative pattern a 'morphogenetic field'.

Sheldrake further suggested that these fields can be subtly changed over time by the form and behaviour of past organisms of the same species - a process he calls 'morphic resonance', which presupposes direct connections (and they would have to be non-physical ones) across time and space.

The implication of what he is saying is that each species of tree, for example, has a formative field on the inner planes which can guide the development of the form of any individual tree so that it has recognisable characteristics. Clearly there are other formative forces, such as local weather, soil and topographical conditions, but the main factor which determines the characteristics of particular species of tree and which distinguishes it from other species is the formative field. Another way we could describe the formative field is as a matrix, a name which also means 'mother'. Indeed, it can be looked at very much as a womb within which the form of the individual unfolds. Of course, each tree is unique, and there is also scope for environmental factors, but if we can see a tree in terms of unfolding within a pre-existing matrix it is a powerful image - and an empowering one.

Creative Energy and Tree Form

So, we have the unity of the universe; the awareness that we and the trees are all part of one being - the living Earth; the existence of all beings, including ourselves and the trees, on many levels of reality; and the presence of formative energies on the subtler levels, which manifest on the physical. These are some of the most basic principles of what might variously be called the magical or esoteric view, shared by many different traditions.

But, what does all this mean in practical terms when we think about trees? Firstly, it provides a depth that is missing from the purely utilitarian viewpoint. Trees are very much part of the living Earth. They have a strong link with others, not just of the same species, but with all trees and, potentially, with ourselves.

Each tree is unique - its precise form of branches, trunk and roots are distinct from every other tree and yet we recognise it as an oak, hawthorn or whatever. It is unique because trees grow according to various underlying fields or matrices, and therefore the form of the tree can reveal the underlying pattern which gave it shape.

Indeed, it is clear that the formative fields are not straightjackets but flexible and respond to the land in which the tree is growing, to its location and environment. It is more like an interaction achieving a unique result - an interaction between its formative energy and the particular factors (seen and unseen) that are present at a place - an expression of nature and nurture, perhaps.

We know very little about these energy fields. They can be felt by many, either directly or using artificial means such as dowsing rods. The results are the interaction between the individual and the site at a particular time. To isolate the factors relating to the site itself as opposed to the percipient and the natural cycles affecting both is very difficult, and it is probably better to accept the existence of energy fields at a site, as a useful concept, without concerning ourselves with too much detail.

As a practical example, unusual tree forms may tell us something about these fields. The unusual has always been considered special or sacred, and tree form is no exception to this, as Nigel Pennick points out:

> "Dowsers have noted that the forms of trees are affected as they grow over underground water, especially blind springs. They develop twisted trunks, double forms and branches grow back into the trunk, making contorted shapes, living indicators of an active place. Twisted trees

35

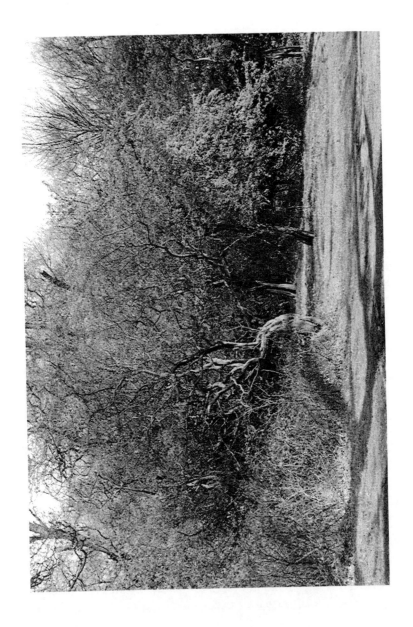

were revered as sacred by the ancient pagans and the spiral wands used by witches and Druids are a reminder of this. As indicators of the character of site, twisted trees are valuable."[92]

When the sensitive, Mary Long, visited Tony Wedd at his home in Chiddingstone, Kent, back in 1960, she was drawn towards a sycamore tree, standing in a wood the other side of his garden wall. The tree had a very pronounced spiral form, and Mary felt that there was a "vortex" at that point, by which she meant the crossover of two important lines of force in the landscape, and that the tree had grown where the actual cross occurred. She noticed that she got a very powerful feeling of energy around it, but not actually at the tree, which she felt rather pointed to its being a vortex.

Mary also had a strong impression that the bark of the sycamore tree had healing properties and that it had to be charred and then infused. I can certainly vouch for this, as Tony gave me a piece of bark, which I filed down into a powder and then infused. It certainly helped a friend who had a skin complaint quite considerably.

Jimmy Goddard has drawn attention to the phenomenon of "double trees" - those with trunks which split very near the ground - occurring on lines of earth energy, which many have found to coincide with leys, as defined by Alfred Watkins.

He cites the example of a double sycamore in Addlestone, Surrey, which leans towards a ley, and a double Scots Pine at the base of a clump through which more than one ley was thought to run. Another tree starts as a double with two trunks in a spiral form round each other, which meet again higher up.

Jimmy continues:

"It is noticeable in several of the clumps that even the trees which are not double or spiral are often twisted into weird shapes or lean in various directions for no apparent reason. It is as if they are buffeted and pushed during their growth by great static waves and whirlpools of energy, caused perhaps by the effects of various features in the landscape on the ley current."39

Nigel Pennick comments:

"Also among unusual hedgerow standards are the mysterious fairy trees, strange hybrids where oak, ash and thorn have grown together by means unknown."92

Wilks refers to a tree at the Woodrow Inn, Cawston in Norfolk:

"... having part beech, part hornbeam and part oak leaves on all its branches, not isolated, but indiscriminately mixed upon every part of the tree."122

He also refers to the way in which trees of different species

"... often embrace each other. A Scots Pine and a beech grow harmoniously trunk to trunk, each enwrapping the other with its branches, at the edge of a clump of tall beeches on the summit of Crichel Down, Dorset. They are locally spoken of as the Two Lovers."122

I also have in my possession a postcard, probably dating from the turn of the century, showing what is described as "Curious Oak and Beech trees growing together, New Forest", which seems to show a common lower trunk with two separate trunks emerging from it.

The Living Aura in Trees

The implication of much of this is that the tree consists of a subtle energy system that we can interact with. One way we can explore this is to think in terms of the aura - the subtle energy which extends out beyond the tree itself and which can be detected by those who are sensitive. The aura may indeed be the detectable manifestation of Sheldrake's formative field.

This is not a static system, but consists of a flow of energy, and it seems reasonably clear from the examples given above that the flow of subtle energy in the earth and within trees affects their form, in some cases quite dramatically.

Many people can sense the aura around trees and at times can become aware of the flow of energy within the tree itself. In general, energy seems to flow up from the earth by way of the roots, up the trunk, and out along the branches and twigs. Some have detected a circular flow and, by standing facing the tree a little way away from the trunk, one can step into this flow so that the energy is completing its cycle by flowing down through your body and back into the earth. This can be a very beneficial exercise, for healing and for increasing your sensitivity to such energies.

The discovery, or rather re-discovery and exploration, of our own subtle anatomy and that of the trees, is really at the stage that knowledge of physical anatomy was at in the Middle Ages before the circulation of blood was discovered.

There is so much that we don't know, and the way forward is, as it always was, to rely on those who are particularly sensitive and can describe what they see. This may be our own direct personal experience, or that of a friend. It may be experience from long ago, now enshrined in folklore, or it may be that the percipient has found a way to express some of their deep experience through artistic expression - poetry, painting, literature or music.

The next chapters will look at people's experience of the spirit of trees as expressed through folklore and art.

Chapter 3

The Tree Spirit in Tradition

"In culture after culture, age after age, the human soul has responded to the spirit of the trees, questioning, and has been answered."
                Pattalee Glass-Koentop - *Year of Moons; Season of Trees*

Trees are the largest beings that have ever existed on the surface of the earth - they are also the longest lived. Even today, in our deforested country, they make an immediate impact. We should therefore not be surprised to find that trees have been important to people, that they have got to know them and have become aware of another dimension in the presence of trees - the sense that there is something more than everyday reality. To put it in different language, people were aware that trees had spirit, and in many cultures this was seen to take on human form and character.

But there are two participants in any communication - in this case, the person and the tree - and people vary enormously in how they experience the spirit of the tree and, it seems, they always have. We will never know of the many who have gained benefit from leaning against a tree, or received comfort and enlightenment from being in the heart of the woods. Many keep such experiences to themselves, either because they feel them to be intensely personal or because they feel unable to express themselves adequately.

It is with those who have spoken out that we are here concerned and it is comforting to me that the subtle qualities of trees are not just some imaginative creation on my part. People have experienced these things throughout time and, particularly in times more amenable to such things than our own, have not kept such experiences to themselves but have communicated them to others in a variety of ways depending on the circumstances.

Seers and Shamans

Perhaps the purest form of link which has been forged between people and trees has been as a result of those special individuals, variously called mystics, seers or shamans, who have what appears to be a natural "open channel" to the higher vibrational level - to what has been called the Otherworld. They have existed in all ages, back to the most ancient of times when people were completely in tune with the land on which they lived.

Not unexpectedly, those cultures where people live close to and in harmony with the land accept the seer as a natural part of their society, for amongst them what we might call the psychic ability is just a normal accepted faculty like the sense of smell. The Australian aborigines, the native Americans, the San people of southern Africa, and the native peoples of Siberia (where the term 'shaman' originated) are just some of the most obvious examples of such cultures. Indeed, there is increasing evidence that in England as recently as the First World War there were people who had a particular affinity with the land, trees and herbs and had special access to the Otherworld. They were the village wise women and cunning men who, in earlier generations, were accused of being witches.

These seers and shamans, from whatever culture they originated, could sense the power and wisdom in a tree and were able to communicate with this spirit of the trees as a gateway to the Otherworld. The Siberian shamans, among others, used to climb trees as part of the initiation process, and as an aid to their spirit flight. The Buddha was not the first to sit under a bodhi tree to await inspiration, and the sacred groves of the Greeks, Romans and Druids were all intended to assist in contact with the Otherworld.

In our own times, there are many who have had the vision, and I pick just three out of those many to illustrate the varied ways that people have perceived the tree spirits.

Dorothy Maclean - Speaking with Angels

Dorothy Maclean had been led, step by step, to help found the community at Findhorn, in northern Scotland. She already realised that she had the ability to "tune in" and receive guidance which she could write down and apply in practical terms.

At Findhorn, they were led to establish a garden to feed themselves and the growing number of visitors. Dorothy found that she could communicate with the spirits of the various plants in the garden and also with the trees. She called these beings 'devas', from the Sanskrit word meaning 'shining one'. They told her much about the underlying energies and spirit with which all plants are endowed, and their guidance enabled the garden at Findhorn to flourish in a remarkable fashion.

Apart from an apple orchard which they had planted, Scots pine were the only large trees on the caravan park where the community was settled. Dorothy Maclean says:

> " ... before the year was out my love of trees had led to a contact with the Scots Pine Deva. There was a strong and

solid feel that distinguished this deva from those of other plants. Confirming my feeling that trees had healing power and much to give to humans, the angel added:

'We are guardians of the Earth in many ways, and humans should be a part of what we guard. We are not active young things; we are, in a way, like a school of benevolent philosophers with unhuman purity and a great wish to serve humanity. Trees are vital to man and to life on this planet, and some of us are eager to experience this contact with some humans before others destroy what we have built up.'"[71]

Later contacts emphasised the need for large trees for the wellbeing of the land, because of the 'inner radiances' which are thus drawn forth. This led them to plant many seedlings around the site.

Some messages from the large-tree devas expressed a feeling of great urgency, that trees need to fulfil themselves and not just be confined to hedges, gardens and single-species plantations.

The Pine Deva of the remnants of the old Caledonian Forest made her realise how people depended on trees spiritually, even though they did not realise it. She perceived that the 'feyness' of the Scot was dying with the old pines and that

"the stalwart and enduring qualities that [the trees] brought to Earth were not appreciated ... this would result in lack of endurance, lack of independence and lack of love of Nature among men."[71]

Dorothy Maclean has received much else from the tree devas. The important thing to note is that such communication is possible and valuable knowledge can be gained as a result. In my own way, I have tried to use these same channels of communication in obtaining material for this book.

Allen Meredith - Dreaming the Yew

One of the chapters in Anand Chetan and Diana Brueton's book *"The Sacred Yew"*[24] is entitled "The Man Who Has Almost Become a Yew Tree" and it tells the story of Allen Meredith and his concern for yews.

It started in 1974, when he was giving a talk about bird-watching to a group of children in Gloucestershire. He was taken to see a yew tree in a nearby churchyard and was told that it was 200 years old. At that moment something inside him told him that it was in fact much older. He didn't know where that feeling came from, but it was very definite.

About a year later, he began to have a series of dreams which revealed to him more about the importance of yew trees, in particular that the yew trees can exist for ever and are a repudiation of death as the end.

These dreams led him to find out as much as he could about yew trees and to campaign to protect them. His studies made him realise that yews were a lot older than had generally been thought - some more than 4000 years old - and this view has gradually taken hold in the scientific establishment.

Kiri Clay-Egerton - Learning from the Tree Spirits

From her youngest days, Kiri Clay-Egerton found trees which taught her much, in their own language:

> *"Many years ago, when I was what I now consider a very impressionable child, I was introduced to (or it was introduced to me: it matters little now) a very large, tall larch tree. It was, in fact, the only tree in a small copse of mixed trees. How it came to be where it was was not mine to question but simply to enjoy. For me it was a gateway to other places and other times. ... The one thing that still*

strikes me is the overpowering sensation of utter stillness and quietness which this old larch radiated over the whole area of the copse. ... This tree I found so pure and calming that to me it became a sacred spot in a place of unlimited beauty. ... This tree gave me an aura of beauty and yet utter solemnity while at the same time providing me with a backrest as I sat peacefully among its gnarled and twisted roots."[26]

Folklore and Mythology

It was a natural step from the recounting of experiences to use trees to represent qualities which people aspired to in the manner which myth, legend and fable have traditionally done so well. And so emerged the telling of stories - some ephemeral, some handed down the generations, some transcribed for posterity.

So those who had particular access to the Otherworld and who could 'see' in a special way, were listened to, and their insights into how the landscape really was became enshrined in tradition.

Tales of experiences are told and, over time, become folklore and mythology, in the process becoming more elaborate and formalised, although originally based on real experience. If properly interpreted, mythology and folklore can give valuable insights into how people saw the natural world, and trees have been a common subject.

It is not my purpose to describe in detail or even give an overview of the folklore associated with trees. This would expand the present volume well beyond its intended size and has already been done very well by a variety of authors, such as Frazer[37]. Rather, I want to look at folklore only insofar as it gives us some insight into the "subtle anatomy" and personality of trees, and our relationships with them. In fact, there is a whole range of mythology, folklore and esoteric teaching which shows both a consistency and a vivid picture of the reality of the subtle aspects of the tree.

One need only examine the work of such writers as Sir James Frazer[37], Mrs Philpot[94] and others to realise the extent to which the mythology and folklore of trees abounds in all parts of the world and from the earliest records. But to be useful it needs to be interpreted, and if we look behind this folklore to the underlying meaning, our task becomes clearer. When we do this, we begin to discern some major themes which have as their focus the way in which trees can act as an intermediary between ourselves and the immensities of the universe. They embody cosmic powers and have the ability to alter our own consciousness accordingly - a recognition of the spiritual nature of trees, that they possess a spirit as we do, and that, under certain circumstances, communication is possible. The major themes that emerge are concerned with life, death and rebirth; the indwelling spirit; oracular vision and healing powers; fertility; and an awareness of our place in the universe.

Tree Worship and the Indwelling Spirit

A lot was written about 'tree worship' by 19th and early 20th Century writers in their studies of native peoples in various parts of the world and of the ancient people of Britain. The problem is that the vast majority of these writers were Christian, or had a Christian background, and therefore, quite naturally, saw things from a Christian perspective. This meant that when they saw, or heard about, people approaching trees with respect, standing before them, addressing words to them and leaving offerings, they interpreted this as 'worship' - an equivalent of the way in which the Christians worshipped their god. In Christian terms, that which was worthy of worship had to be all-powerful and transcendent, and therefore they assumed that the pagans felt the same about their trees, springs, rocks or whatever.

They did not!

What the pagans were doing, in making offerings etc. to the trees, was to recognise the indwelling spirit, to respect it, and to acknowledge that they were all equally part of a living Earth. So, many practices that were interpreted as 'tree worship' were nothing of the sort, though there was respect, and even awe. What was being worshipped was the spirit which manifests within the tree rather than the tree itself, just as Christians do not worship the various artifacts found within their churches.

From an esoteric point of view, it is clear that these tales originate from a very real perception of the indwelling spirit present in all trees. Some people could under certain conditions sense this spirit and they interpreted it in terms which could be understood by their own culture. Thus we get tree gods and tree goddesses, nature spirits, dryads and the like which, in accordance with human nature, had legend, folklore and mythology grow up around them. The life in the tree was seen in most times and places in terms of living beings - gods, goddesses, dryads, wood-spirits, elves, etc. This is because we have a tendency to do this - to anthropo-morphise what are essentially tree beings in their own right with their own characteristics.

It was central to many traditions to recognise that each tree had a spirit living within it. This was reflected in a great respect for trees and a consequent belief that bad luck would ensue if you cut one down, unless the spirit was propitiated in some way, perhaps with offerings and certainly with an apology. Indeed, to fell a tree was a very serious offence, in some places punishable by death.

In ancient Greece, these spirits were known as dryads. Originally they were the nymphs of oak trees, but the term was later applied to all tree spirits. Indeed, most cultures have stories of spirits which live in trees.

This indwelling spirit has also been characterised as the Man in the Trees or the Green Man, as John Fowles reminds us:

> *"One of the oldest and most diffused bodies of myth and folklore has accreted round the idea of the man in the trees. In all his manifestations, as dryad, as stag-headed Herne, as outlaw, he possesses the characteristic of elusiveness, a power of 'melting' into the trees, and I am certain the attraction of the myth is so profound and universal because it is constantly 'played' inside every individual consciousness."*[36]

Symbols of Regeneration and Resurrection

We have seen how trees live far longer than human beings, so that an individual oak or yew will stand relatively unchanged while generations of people are born, live and die. And the trees themselves exhibit ways of regeneration which means that some of them, like the yew, can continue their life apparently for ever. These qualities are the underlying truth behind many legends and much mythology and folklore.

The Phrygian myth of Attis is a good example. He was a vegetation god and his mother, Nana, conceived him by placing a ripe almond or pomegranate in her bosom. Later in life, he castrated himself under a pine tree and bled to death on the spot. After his death, he is said to have been changed into a pine tree himself.

At the spring festival on 22nd March (the equinox) a pine tree was cut in the woods, brought into a sanctuary, and was swathed like a corpse and treated as a divinity. Three days later, Attis is said to have risen from his tomb, amongst much celebration.

There are several points to note in this myth. Apart from clearly being the model upon which the Christian events of Easter are based, it shows the true nature of the tree spirits, in that Attis had to divest himself of any male trappings before becoming a tree spirit himself. In other words, tree spirits have transcended the differences between male and female, incorporating both qualities of yin and yang within themselves, a major theme running like a thread through many ancient esoteric traditions.

The roots of yew trees in churchyards are traditionally said to seek out the bodies which are buried there, the immortality of those individuals being symbolised by the transmutation of their bodies into the immortal yew. In China, Frazer says:

> "... it has been customary from time immemorial to plant trees on graves in order thereby to strengthen the soul of the deceased and thus to save his body from corruption; and as the evergreen cypress and pine are deemed to be fuller of vitality than other trees, they have been chosen by preference for this purpose."[37]

Trees of Passage

Trees have often been seen, not just as the dwelling-places of spirits, but as places to which the being of the deceased individual withdraws before passing over to the Otherworld. Perhaps this is one reason for the planting of trees in churchyards. The sycamore fig of Egypt was one of these, as Pattalee Glass-Koentop recounts:

> "The sycamore fig of Egypt sheltered Osiris, god of the dead and also Hathor, the mother goddess. These trees

were believed to grow at the boundaries of the vast desert and the afterworld. It was said that the deities of those trees gave sustenance to the departing soul as it traveled to the next world."[38]

Some cultures have taken these ideas further and adopted tree burial, taking literally the image of "the souls of the dead climbing the trees, the home of the gods, to reach paradise". In some cases, the souls of the dead are supposed to inhabit trees on a permanent basis, as Frazer recounts:

"The Dieri tribe of Central Australia regard as very sacred certain trees which are supposed to be their fathers transformed; hence they speak with reverence of these trees, and are careful that they shall not be cut down or burned. ... Some of the Philippine Islanders believe that the souls of their ancestors are in certain trees, which they therefore spare. ... The spirits take up their abode, by preference, in tall and stately trees with great spreading branches. When the wind rustles the leaves, the natives fancy it is the voice of the spirit; and they never pass near one of these trees without bowing respectfully and asking pardon of the spirit for disturbing his repose."[37]

Trees as Oracles

Trees have a wisdom and a knowledge that, in certain circumstances, can be tapped into, and this wisdom of the trees has been acknowledged from ancient times. Traditionally, secrets were told to the trees, as they were to bees, so that their oracular function was, in a sense, a two-way process.

The methods by which oracular guidance was given are less clear but could have involved direct-voice communication, the interpretation of the sounds of the wind in the trees while in an altered state of consciousness, and what is known as "dream incubation", where dreams obtained at the site are interpreted for meaning.

The oak grove at Dodona, in Greece, is a good example of such an oracular site. It survived for over 2000 years and was known as "the place of the talking oak trees". These trees were in a group which formed a sacred grove. Originally it was sacred to the Goddess and it is perhaps significant that Frazer records that:

> "... a spring is said to have gushed from the foot of the great oak at Dodona, and from its murmurous flow the priestess drew oracles."[37]

In this connection, Jimmy Goddard has noted the similarity in pitch between the sound of running water and the sound of wind blowing through the trees.

In later times, the grove became sacred to Zeus, and his priests, when they wanted answers, purified themselves (presumably in the sacred spring), and then went to the grove, where the trees spoke with human voices. Zeus is said to have inhabited one particular oak tree, which became known as the oracular oak. Frazer records that:

> "The thunderstorms which are said to rage at Dodona more frequently than anywhere else in Europe, would render the spot a fitting home for the god whose voice was heard alike in the rustling of the oak leaves and in the crash of thunder."[37]

Paul Devereux takes this idea further:

> "The voice of Zeus could be heard at Dodona, and was consulted by Odysseus. At that time the site was probably just a great sacred oak, and Jaynes suggests that the voice was stimulated hallucinogenically from 'the wind

trembling in its leaves' and wonders if the oaks of the Druids may have acted as similar stimuli. In the fifth century BC, Zeus could no longer be heard directly, and there had to be a priestess who spoke for the god while in trance."[34]

Other oracular trees are known from many different cultures, including Persia, Arabia, Armenia and Lithuania.

The Tree as Healer

Much folklore surrounds the healing function of trees in general, as well as the particular qualities of certain individuals. It is certain that in most cultures trees were a centre for healing, both as a source of therapeutic materials and medicinal ingredients, and as a place of pilgrimage and prayer. I have devoted Chapter 12 to this important function of trees.

Identification and Intimacy with the Tree

Sex and fertility were important parts of life in ancient times, and trees, because of their own qualities, became symbols for them. One need only look at the maypole to see the truth of this. As Andrew Morton says:

> *"Early rituals including tree rituals were often intended to ensure fertility and little distinction was made between human fertility and the fertility of the earth, perhaps a reflection of the oneness of man and nature."*[87]

We have already noted that most trees have both male and female flowers and this state of sexual fulfilment, where the qualities of both sexes are fully attained, is one of the teachings with which trees can most readily be identified. This is symbolically represented by such stories as that of Philemon and Baucis, two lovers who, at their deaths, were turned into an oak and a linden. These trees grew so close to each other that their branches intertwined just as Philemon and Baucis had held each other close when alive. Indeed, in some parts of the world, such as Germany, the male and female trees were sometimes married to each other.

Yvonne Aburrow tells us certain legends which link person, tree and fertility together. She says that there is:

> "... the recurring image of the woman and tree in Prakit and Sanskrit texts. It is known as the Salabhanjia: a pose of a woman pulling down the branch of a tree ... salabhanjia is a classic pose in Indian art for depicting tree-goddesses, which may have served as models for the nativity pose of Queen Maya, the mother of Buddha. The pose consists of one arm bending down the branch, the opposite leg crooked round the trunk of the tree, and the other foot resting among the roots of the tree. ... In Buddhist art, the salabhanjia often represents Maya, the mother of Buddha, pulling down the branch of a Sala tree at Lumbini to induce labour ... In modern India there is a children's game called coriya nuki ... in which several children chase a girl until she reaches a tree and touches its trunk, then bends down a branch. If she lets go they can 'take her prisoner' but if not she is 'protected' by the tree. ... There is also the tradition of Dohada, the fertilisation of trees by pregnant women, which found its way into the Koran with the legend of Mary the mother of Christ sitting under a palm tree which Allah then made fertile, and thence into various songs and legends of Europe."[3]

Frazer, writing about the sacred grove of Diana, refers to the line of priests who served under the title of Rex Nemorensis (Kings of the Wood):

"It is natural, therefore, to conjecture that they stood to the goddess of the grove in the same relation in which Virbius stood to her; in short, that the mortal King of the Wood had for his queen the woodland Diana herself. If the sacred tree which he guarded with his life was supposed, as seems probable, to be her special embodiment, her priest may not only have worshipped it as his goddess but embraced it as his wife. There is at least nothing absurd in the supposition, since even in the time of Pliny a noble Roman used thus to treat a beautiful beech-tree in another sacred grove of Diana on the Alban hills. He embraced it, he kissed it, he lay under its shadow, he poured wine on its trunk. Apparently he took the tree for the goddess. The custom of physically marrying men and women to trees is still practised in India and other parts of the East"[37]

Pagans, of course, still hug and kiss trees, lie in their shade and pour offerings of wine over their trunk.

Acknowledging the Tree as a Symbol for the Universe

The qualities which trees possess - longevity, inner strength and flexibility, the ability to regenerate and the way they link earth and sky - have made them particularly suitable to act as symbols which help in an understanding of the universe around us. Indeed, the tree functions as an archetype, and in many cultures we get the World Tree and the Tree of Life, and variants on these, which symbolise the way in which we relate to the rest of the Universe in both space and time.

The word 'tree' is used in everyday life, to describe things which branch or have roots, such as 'family trees'. It is also used as a symbol to represent areas of thought or knowledge where things are not completely structured, but they can conveniently be thought of as having roots, a trunk and

branches. The use of tree symbolism helps to structure these thoughts and indicates that the tripartite structure of the tree (roots, trunk and branches) has parallels in many other spheres. We also use the names for the parts of trees in many aspects of our daily life, and we need only think of seeds (particularly acorns), leaves, fruit, flowers, branches, roots and trunk to realise the truth of such a statement. In other words, trees are important to us and they have not only permeated our language but have, perhaps even more significantly, influenced the way we perceive and structure the world around us.

The tree is frequently visualised as the central pivot upon which the world revolves. Such a concept is found in the legends of many cultures, from that of the Siberian shaman to those of Greece, Persia, Chaldea and Japan. This has been called the axis mundi - a symbol of the unity of the universe by the joining of the earth to the sky and to the underworld as a manifestation of that unity. Alby Stone[105] calls it "the place where it is possible to gain admittance to or communicate with the otherworlds, the realms of the gods or the spirits of the dead". It is actually a physical representation of the symbolic truth that we are at the centre of the universe.

This symbol occurs in traditional Indo-European cosmologies, being the link between the omphalos, or centre point of the earth in any locality, and the centre point of the sky, the Pole Star around which the wheel of the heavens revolves. These are clearly not in physical terms the same axis, but the link is made because of the similarity of their functions. It was often represented by a tree, such as the Norse world-tree, Yggdrasil, or a pillar such as the Irminsul, sacred to the Saxons until destroyed by Charlemagne in 772CE. The turning of the cosmic mill, or the well at the centre of the world, were also used as symbols.

Yggdrasil is probably the most familiar to us. The essence of the tree, which is usually represented as an ash, although some have suggested a yew, is that it joins the different worlds (in other words, planes of existence). Its detailed description contains much rich symbolism. It is the tree of existence, symbolising life, time and destiny, with its roots in the kingdom of death, being watered from the sacred well by the three fates of past, present and future. This is the tree on which Odin is said to have hung for nine days and nights to obtain the wisdom of the runes.

The mystical Hebrew tradition of the Qabalah is often called 'The Tree of Life'. Essentially it is a structural system for understanding the universe and has a very rich symbolism. It consists of locations and paths between them and has been described as a tree with its roots in the reality of spirit and its branches in the illusion of physical existence.

Folklore continues into the present day, but the subject matter of its equivalent - what Paul Screeton calls 'urban belief tales' - is generally of a more artificial environment than trees. And yet, trees remain part of our 'culture of the imagination'. Literature abounds with references to trees and they are a favourite subject for art. In the next chapter, we explore the contribution which trees have made to art in its widest sense.

Chapter 4

The Tree Spirit in Art

"We are all poets when we are in the pine woods."
N.T. Mirov and J. Hasbrouck

Vision leads on to action: Buddha taught the basics of what has become a world religion, Dorothy Maclean's contact with the devas resulted in prolific growth in the Findhorn Garden, and Allen Meredith's dreams have resulted in a campaign to save the yews.

And one important result of vision is artistic expression. Art has always occupied that space between the spiritual and the purely practical. It shows the way, potentially opening the doors of perception to other realms. We should not therefore be surprised that the qualities possessed by trees have made them natural subjects for art in all its forms - including literature, poetry, painting, photography, sculpture and music.

Movement and the Upward Line

Even the most representational of art seems to involve bringing through something from the Otherworld into everyday reality. With trees, it often seems to be that the artist, consciously or unconsciously, is aware of the energy flows through the body of the tree, echoing these movements with movements of the brush, pen, or whatever is being used in the expression of the particular art form. The artist, Irene Coates, now living in Australia, refers to the upward brush stroke in painting, expressing the life force which flows in all of us and which opposes gravity. She links this particularly with the energies which women express, though it is applicable to all whose subject is the living world[27].

Looked at in this way, trees are a living expression of the life force of the earth, and they show its flow and direction in their form. This has been recognised by many of those who have made trees a major focus of their work. Indeed, there are at least three movements taking place in trees including the upward movement of growth which Irene Coates has observed and the natural expression of that upward movement in painting.

There is also the movement of the wind. The wind itself is invisible and is only made manifest in the movement of things which it touches. Trees are in a unique position here. Rocks and houses are rarely moved by the wind, whereas clouds float and change form at the whim of the wind before being dispersed and gone for ever. Trees, in contrast, are rooted in the ground and yet it is by the movement of their leaves, twigs and branches that the wind is brought to our view. This is a rich subject for meditation, but also provides some difficulty for the artist, as Hugh Casson relates:

> "Trees are more difficult to draw than buildings. They don't stand still and their intricate structure demands very careful study which few of us are conscientious enough to undertake. To draw them well you have to take trouble. My advice is Ruskin's, 'Don't look at them, watch them'."[123]

This distinction between looking and watching is an interesting one. Watching implies a period of time - slowing down our activity to more closely coincide with that of the tree. Indeed, those who have ever tried drawing will testify to the fact that it is a useful exercise in observation if nothing else, in that you really have to not just see something but notice it and observe it in order to draw it effectively. To draw, however inadequately, necessitates really seeing something and, moreover, remembering it.

Landscape Painting

Trees have always formed an important element in landscape painting. Chris Titterington notes the prevalence of trees in mythology and says that:

> *"Given this centrality to our myth-forming intelligence it is perhaps inevitable that trees should appear as frequent subjects in our representations of ourselves and the world we inhabit."*[108]

He also notes that their vertical linearity is useful in the composition of a picture. This seems to be another expression of Irene Coates' upward line' - the movement against gravity (which is the origin of the mythology of the Universal Tree) and which underlies much great architecture, notably the Gothic cathedrals. Sir George Trevelyan explains what is happening in such buildings:

> *"As an emotional experience, matter is being lifted and dematerialized. The higher it is raised from earth the more it is dissolved. It is being metamorphosed into even subtler forms until it passes back into the higher planes of energy, 'being', spirit. Thus we must feel that where it dematerializes the energy moves on to an ethereal plane."*[109]

If this is achieved in great architecture, how much more so is it inherent in the trees themselves, which stood as a model for such buildings?

The geographer, Jay Appleton, enquiring into the aesthetics of landscape, asked two very simple questions: "What do we like about landscape and why do we like it?"[6] Like all the best questions, they led in surprising and fruitful directions. He found a passage from Konrad Lorenz' "King Solomon's Ring", which provided a valuable clue:

> *"It is early one morning at the beginning of March, when Easter is already in the air, and we are taking a walk in the forest whose wooded slopes of tall beeches can be equalled in beauty by few and surpassed by none. We approach a forest glade. The tall smooth trunks of the beeches give place to the hornbeam which are dotted from top to bottom with pale green foliage. We now tread slowly and more carefully. Before we break through the last bushes and out of cover on to the free expanse of the meadow, we do what all wild animals and all good naturalists, wild boars, leopards, hunters and zoologists would do under similar circumstances: we reconnoitre, seeking, before we leave our cover, to gain from it the advantage which it can offer alike to hunter and hunted - namely to see without being seen."[65]*

What Appleton did was to make the connection between the advantages for survival of both seeing and hiding and the attractiveness which we feel for particular landscapes. He goes on to develop what he calls Prospect/Refuge Theory. A prospect dominant landscape would be one with many hills, escarpments, cliffs and prominences which provided plenty of sites where one could experience vistas and panoramas: a refuge dominant landscape would have plenty of dark hiding places, such as narrow valleys, sheltered crevices and woodland.

He found that traditional landscape painting frequently made use of such imagery, which often incorporated trees, both as a refuge (for example, a dark wood) and as indicating a prospect (a solitary pine at the top of a hill).

Trees certainly play a valuable role in landscape painting, as Titterington has pointed out, and Appleton's insights have shown what that attraction of trees might be, whether as a refuge (both individual tree and forest) or as emphasising a vantage point.

This latter is well illustrated by a copy of a painting by Sutton Palmer RA that I found in a junk shop which I had framed and now adorns one of the few areas of wall in my room not covered with bookshelves! It is a view of the Eden Valley in Cumberland, the river running in a steep gorge, with tall Scots pines growing on the edge of a cliff overlooking the river. The painting would be so much less interesting without the trees, which give it a strong dramatic quality. Woods, to which Chapter 8 is devoted, are however a very different matter, as John Fowles has observed:

> *"In a way woods are like the sea, sensorily far too various and immense for anything but surfaces or glimpses to be captured. They defeat view finder, drawing-paper, canvas, they cannot be framed; and words are as futile, hopelessly too laborious and used to capture the reality."[36]*

In fact, woods have been successfully painted, but it is nearly always the spaces in the forest, such as paths or glades rather than the woodland depths themselves, which are featured. Indeed, another painting by Sutton Palmer, entitled "Woodland Depths, Wotton" actually turns out to be a view of trees across a stretch of open water!

Sculpture and Carving

Buildings are, to some extent, a retreat from Nature. We are, or like to think we are, in control. And yet, we are not completely apart from Nature. We welcome it in, but in concrete form, simplified, tamed and polished.

65

Before the advent of Christianity in this country, much pagan worship and ritual was in the open air - within and surrounded by Nature, something that was instinctively felt to be right. As church building increased, the people (who saw no reason to abandon their paganism just because they had espoused Christianity, seeing no incompatibility between the two) naturally started to decorate their churches with pagan symbols - a reminder of the greenwood and the old gods.

Many of these carvings had the tree as a central feature, and foliage predominated. It is interesting that the oak leaf and the acorn are probably the most common, as these are the particular sacred trees of the Old Religion, dating back at least to the time of the Druids. Complete tree forms also appear, particularly on fonts, and these are, rather loosely, described as 'The Tree of Life'. Also prominent are foliate heads, also often called The Green Man. These have vegetation actually coming out of the mouth, flowing in often highly elaborate forms.

The point about these carvings (and others, with specifically sexual themes, such as the Sheila-na-Gig, which are beyond the scope of this book) is that they all have explanations in Christian iconography, so that the clergy of the day would be satisfied, but it is quite clear that they had an older, pagan, meaning as well. They were really there as symbols to remind the people that Nature was present outside, and to keep the trees, with all their vitality, in their minds and hearts while they were indoors.

The Tree in Literature

Trees feature prominently in literature, as they do in the landscape. I do not have the knowledge or space to attempt any sort of overview, and would refer the interested reader to Kim Taplin's book "Tongues in Trees"[107], which looks at the works of some authors in some depth. Essentially the tree performs the same function in literature as it does in landscape painting - it provides a setting, in both space and time, for human existence.

In particular, the wood is there as a background for human activity, whether it is Knyghtwood in *"The Herb of Grace"*, Yalbury Wood in *"Under the Greenwood Tree"*, or, indeed, the eponymous setting of *"Under Milk Wood"*. We shall be looking at the insights that some literature has shed on the spirits of the wood in Chapter 8.

From the legends and stories of Robin Hood to the works of Thomas Hardy, the wood is always there. Yet Kim Taplin reminds us that Hardy did not just see the wood in idyllic terms. *"Under the Greenwood Tree"* and *"The Woodlanders"* certainly present a picture of humanity in harmony with the woods and trees. Written towards the end of the 19th Century, they are perhaps the end of an era stretching back to prehistoric times. But threats to the woods were present even before Hardy's time, and there has always been a certain ambivalence towards the wood, which is well illustrated in Kenneth Grahame's *"The Wind in the Willows"*, describing the Mole's venture into the Wild Wood:

> *"There was nothing to alarm him at first entry. Twigs crackled under his feet, logs tripped him, funguses on stumps resembled caricatures, and startled him for the moment by their likeness to something familiar and far away; but that was all fun, and exciting. It led him on, and he penetrated to where the light was less, and trees crouched nearer and nearer, and holes made ugly mouths at him on either side.*
>
> *Everything was very still now. The dusk advanced on him steadily, rapidly, gathering in behind and before; and the light seemed to be draining away like flood-water."[41]*

Then faces, whistling and pattering began:

> *"The pattering increased till it sounded like sudden hail on the dry-leaf carpet spread around him. The whole wood seemed running now, running hard, hunting, chasing, closing in round something or - somebody? In panic, he began to run too, aimlessly, he knew not whither. He ran up against things, he fell over things and into things, he darted under things and dodged round things. At last he took refuge in the deep dark hollow of an old beech tree, which offered shelter, concealment - perhaps even safety, but who could tell? Anyhow, he was too tired to run any further and could only snuggle down into the dry leaves which had drifted into the hollow and hope he was safe for the time. And as he lay there panting and trembling, and listened to the whistlings and the patterings outside, he knew it at last, in all its fullness, that dread thing which other little dwellers in field and hedgerow had encountered here, and known as their darkest moment - that thing which the Rat had vainly tried to shield him from - the Terror of the Wild Wood!"*[41]

We shall be looking further at this ambivalence of feelings towards the wood in Chapter 8.

Poetry

Several collections of poems about trees have been published, including *"Touch Wood"* by Herbert Whone[120], *"Spirit of the Trees"* by Ruth Alston Cresswell[31], and Angela King and Sue Clifford's *"Trees be Company"*[56].

Herbert Whone is a musician, and his book, which is subtitled *"A Journey Among Trees"*, is a collection of poetry and prose on all aspects of trees, which is illustrated by some of his own photographs, which are full of life and capture the spirit and energy of the trees very well. The poems and text collected by him for the book are remarkable and give vivid confirmation that others have seen the spirit resident in the trees and have described it most eloquently.

Indeed, it seems almost as if the quality of poetry and the character of trees go very easily together, for a large proportion of published poetry seems devoted to the subject. Poets have had deep insights into the nature of trees and I have gained from and used these insights throughout the book. Poetry allies itself with trees, for they are, in some strange way, similar beings. Kim Taplin gives some explanation for this:

> "It is only art, and perhaps poetry in particular, that can bring terrible things home to us without causing us to despair. Its consoling power lies in its affirmation of the possibility of rebirth and regeneration. It in some way participates in the renewing sustaining power of the earth itself. Part of poetry's function is the reminding us, magically, what is our relationship to the earth. Robert Graves went so far as to suggest, in The White Goddess (1948) that it was its sole true function."[107]

Trees and Photography

Trees are still, yet moving - as a subject, half way between still life and action photography. In taking photographs of trees, various hints, as from explorers, are given from time to time. Frank Horvat, for example, avoids any human artifacts, making the tree the central focus. I have often found that the mists of early morning are good for distinguishing the trees one from another, fading from clear dark limbs into the unity of distance, the cover of "Touch Wood" giving a good example of this.

My own photographs are often of parts of trees - trunk, branch or root, or of what I call locations - showing the relationship between trees and their surrounding landforms - rather than just the trees themselves.

Alfred Watkins, the discoverer of leys, was a master at this sort of thing, particularly in the context of illustrating the old straight tracks. He used trees almost unconsciously to 'frame' the photograph, remarking that the best photographs were taken along the line of the ley.

Frank Horvat has some revealing comments to make on the possible function of the photograph from the point of view of the tree:

> *"The spectacle of these stationary beings, creeping into space by a movement of growth, yet unable to move in any other way, seems to me to contain a lesson we cannot afford not to learn; and at the same time, paradoxically, to pass our understanding. It is as if the parasites on their bodies - including ourselves - were no more than instruments invented by trees to serve their immobility.*
>
> *If thought is an abstract form of movement, the photographic approach, in which I have used trees to express a part of myself, must be an abstract form of this parasitism. One could even imagine that the tree, static yet omnipotent, has used my parasitic camera to extend its branches into the mental space of the common imagination."*[36]

Chapter 5

Towards Communion

"Whoever has learned how to listen to trees no longer wants to be a tree. He wants to be nothing except what he is. That is home. That is happiness."

Hermann Hesse - *Wandering*

'Talking to Trees' has become one of those almost archetypal activities which, in the public mind, characterises what has become known as the 'New Age'. Like the use of that other archetype, the crystal ball, it is a genuine technique, but it is, at most, only half the story. More important than talking to trees is listening to them. If we want to build up a relationship with trees then we should act as we would in any other meaningful relationship - to listen as well as to talk.

We have seen that people have listened to trees in many different ways - the Buddha sat overnight under the bodhi tree, Dorothy Maclean stilled her mind and allowed the messages to flow, and Allen Meredith climbed the ancient yews and fell asleep to dream.

It is a matter of confidence. If we want to make contact with the spirit of the trees, we probably have enough instinctive awareness to do the right thing. But it is always comforting to know how others have approached it, and I will give a few hints which you are at liberty to accept or reject as you wish.

If you find them useful, that is fine. If you want to go your own way, that is equally fine.

This is, of course, a two-way process - we may be 'talking to' the trees (or communicating our feelings in some other way), or we may be listening to them - trying to pick up some impression. There is also a third state - which is actually beyond both talking and listening which can perhaps best be described as 'complete identification with the tree', and I give hints on ways of attaining this state.

We have already seen how people have lived with trees as an important part of their everyday experience, and how they have become aware of a deeper dimension to a tree or, in other words, they have found its spirit. This chapter is intended as a guide in getting to know trees at this deeper level. I will suggest certain general principles, but the most important thing is to use your intuition about what is right. Everyone has their own way of receiving impressions, perhaps visually, or in words, or through their emotional or bodily feelings. What matters is that we find what works for us and put our trust in it.

Why?

But why should we want to get to know trees at a deep level?

Perhaps the best and most honest answer is because we feel we want to. There is no need for rationalising, because rationality is absent at the deeper levels, or rather it is a different sort of rationality.

But there is also an underlying feeling that trees possess wisdom of a quality unknown to ourselves. They are older, in many cases far older, than we are and they have accumulated the fruits of experience to which, at the deeper level, we can gain access.

Then again, their very longevity and fixity means they have something to teach us about patience and slowing our activity down. This very quality can be unbearable to us if we are exposed to too much of it, for we are active beings, always moving about and doing things. The sense of being and centredness surrounding a tree is attractive for a time, but there comes a point where we begin to long for a change of scene and a return to our busy activity. But, to attune to the slower rhythms of a tree, even for a short period, can be most beneficial to our whole being.

It may be that we have some specific question or problem that we want an answer to and, as we saw in the last chapter, the oracular power of trees has long been known and used.

Trees are also great healers. To turn to the woods and trees for solace is one of the oldest and most natural of activities. We can be cheered, life can be put in perspective, and we can come back stronger and more able to deal with the pressures of everyday life.

Indeed, trees can help with our own spiritual development, helping to achieve changes in consciousness, and thus giving a wider and deeper perspective on our lives.

So, I set out a series of stages in communicating with a tree. Use them as a guide only. You might want to spend little time on one stage and a lot on another. You might carry them out in a different order, or even omit some of them altogether. This doesn't matter - what matters is what works for you. This is merely a guide to get you started.

Take Time

Trees are much slower than we are. They stay in one place and, apart from the effect of the wind on their leaves and branches, they appear to change at a much slower rate than our second-to-second alterations in facial appearance, mood and other activities.

Many of us lead very busy lives, with meetings, appointments and other things we need to get done. It is difficult to escape from these completely, but we need to try to reduce the time-pressure on ourselves when we want to attune with a tree. If we are always looking at our watch, being anxious that we might be late for our next appointment, we will find it very difficult to relax sufficiently and to slow our pace down to approach that of the tree. So, try to give yourself a reasonable period of time, preferably a whole day, so that you can then forget about time and concentrate fully on communicating with the trees. For what we are trying to do is to slow down our rhythms and mental activity in an attempt to approach more nearly the rate at which the tree is living so that communication becomes possible. Writing of the rowan, Heather Blamires says:

> "... the most important information to be gleaned from this beautiful tree can only be "felt" by spending time with her and learning on a purely emotive level from her presence. No written description can compensate for this special communication."[13]

Finding your Place

Most of us have trees within a short distance of where we live and, in one sense, we can relate to any tree in the way I am about to describe, if we really want to. However, thinking of ourselves as much as the tree, we can often attune more easily if we are a little way apart from the public realm. In writing about communicating with nature spirits, Morgan Raven gives the following advice, which is equally applicable to trees:

> "When you're first attempting this form of communication you'll find it much easier to start off in

some place which is remote from human affairs. Find somewhere where humans have made as little impact on the environment as possible. A mountainside or moorland is probably the best in this country but if you don't have easy access to such a place don't let this stop you from having a go at communicating with nature spirits. If you can find nowhere else use your own garden, preferably a part where you allow wild plants and grasses to grow as they will or try a public park. It may well be more difficult in places such as these but it isn't impossible."[99]

If we are able to manage it, a walk through a wood is ideal, in that there are plenty of trees and it is easier to escape from other people. But it is not essential. Trees on a piece of "waste land" behind a factory or on a railway embankment can function just as well. In fact, if you have got this far in reading this book, you will almost certainly already know some trees that are special to you and, as Yvonne Aburrow has pointed out, if you walk through a wood enough times, you begin to be aware of which trees are most powerful.

The fresh air and physical exercise of walking will help to put you in the right frame of mind. The principle of *solvitur ambulando* ("you can work it out by walking") can apply and we can find our worries and anxieties falling away, at least temporarily.

This walking is not intended necessarily to be vigorous exercise, covering as much ground in as short a time as possible. Indeed, the intention is to notice our surroundings and, for this, as the great geographer Carl O. Sauer used to say, "Locomotion should be slow - the slower the better". Indeed, it is really a form of walking meditation, where the rhythms of the walking combine with the rhythms of the breathing and the brainwaves to induce a meditative state.

Simon Lilly gives an indication of what you might be feeling:

> *"If you start to become aware of your subtle feelings you will soon notice that different trees or different woods, copses or groups of a single type of tree will alter your consciousness. This will be caused by the differences to the senses, different smell, light, sounds and so on but not only these, there will be an underlying mental "feel". If you allow yourself to tune into this and allow yourself to express it in a language your conscious mind will understand you will gradually be able to pinpoint what is going on at an energy or vibrational level."[63]*

So, go to somewhere that you are drawn to, and it will almost certainly be the right place for you.

Dowsing with your Feet

The objective now is to move through the area and to do this as slowly as possible, in a state of walking meditation, where you are consciously clearing your mind to allow impressions to register, and where your slow but rhythmical form of walking induces a certain state of mind, difficult to describe but easy to recognise when it is achieved, where one is in a state of what might be called "relaxed readiness".

What you are aiming to do is to choose a tree, or rather to become aware of when a tree has chosen you. You will be moving slowly, perhaps keeping to the path, perhaps wandering off into the undergrowth. It is a funny thing, but if you are in this particular state you will find that roots will not trip you up, brambles will not scratch and you will be able to move through between trees and under branches in a harmonious way. It is, in fact, a sign as to whether you are fully in tune. Don't worry unduly if you are not - just stand still and allow the feeling to grow again.

I have called this sort of thing "dowsing with your feet" because it seems to have much in common with water-divining (or dowsing) with a forked hazel twig to find water. Only on this occasion your objective is to find a tree.

Recognition and Approach

You will find your tree. At some stage in your walk you will find your tree. Don't worry if one doesn't spring out to greet you. You are probably the sort of person who (like me) finds it difficult to make up their mind. It's just that you've been very observant and have noticed several trees which seem attractive.

But now, you have to choose just one. Choose one. It doesn't matter how silly the basis on which you choose it is - you needn't tell anyone else. You will choose one, and it will be the right tree for you at that time, and it will have the qualities you need on that occasion.

Just allow yourself to be attracted to one particular tree, allowing your intuition to lead you. It might help to see it in terms of the tree choosing you. In other words, you don't have to do anything. Forget about the difficult task of choosing - you are going to be chosen, and it is just a question of looking out for when that happens. Being chosen is a lot easier than having to choose!

Stand still for a moment, just looking at the tree. Observe it. See if you can name the species, but don't worry if you can't. Remember, the tree doesn't know itself by that name! See how it stands relative to the other trees. Look at it and its surroundings until you know that you could find it and recognise it again.

This is not just for your benefit - the tree needs time to become aware of what you are thinking and feeling, which it will do, since trees are generally far more sensitive than we are. Incidentally, this is another reason why it is a good idea to let the tree choose you - that way, the tree will already be aware of your presence, and it will be easier to build upon some level of relationship since, in a sense, the tree has made the first step. In reality it is more a matter of mutual recognition. But take time with this stage. Just stand still, try to still your mind, and observe what is going on.

Trees are mature and wise beings. The tree that you wish to communicate with is likely to be older than you are - perhaps considerably older - and, in order to be on good terms with them, we need to treat them with respect. And this means asking permission to approach them. I'm not saying that we need to do this every time we walk through a wood, just as we wouldn't when walking along a crowded street, but I think things are different when we have picked out a particular tree and wish to form a closer acquaintance with it.

Asking permission is highly significant - it is not just a formality, even when you feel that the tree has chosen you - so, when you feel sufficiently attuned, make the request in your mind - ask if the tree would have any objection to you approaching it more closely and tuning in to it.

You can ask for some sort of sign, but don't worry if you don't feel you are getting any response from the tree. More than likely you will not get the answer as a blinding flash. If you ask clearly in your mind, you will be feeling a response at a deeper level and you will find yourself acting accordingly. What will probably happen is that you will, of your own accord, start to approach the tree more closely or find yourself walking away. That, in fact, is your answer, if you asked the question with an open mind, perfectly prepared to receive the answer "no". In fact, in most cases, the tree will welcome you - if not with open arms then certainly with open roots and branches.

There may be occasions, however, when the tree may not want your attention. It may be that it has undergone stress or trauma in the recent past (recent to the tree, that is), perhaps as a result of disease, excessive grazing or vandalism such as lopping of branches or leaves. This can result in a depletion of its energy and it would not be right to exploit further a tree in that condition. The most you should do in such a case is to direct some healing energy to the tree and then leave it in peace.

Don't hurry towards the tree - it is a living being and, whilst it can't run away like an animal, it will be sensitive to your approach, which is thus best done in a gentle, non-threatening way. Try to slow your functioning down and psychically root yourself in the earth, so that you can approach the tree more on its own terms.

Peter Aziz recommends approaching trees quietly, and with respect. He also advises approaching from the north "as it is more sensitive on the side where the sun never shines."[7] This is usually the side where the trunk is greenest with moss and algae.

As you approach the tree, keep sensitive to its presence, and note any changes of feelings as you get nearer. At some point you will begin to feel the presence of the tree in a different way, as you enter its aura, and you will be truly standing within the tree's own space. You may feel the edge of the aura as a definite barrier that requires some effort to cross, like walking through a spider's web, or you may experience a warm, welcoming feeling enveloping your whole body. Different people experience the aura in different ways. Most of us will notice some change in what we feel: others can even see the aura and the fine and delicate energy flows that make it up. You may notice that the aura has several layers which can be felt as you approach the tree. Some have noted as many as five, but don't worry if you can't experience them all.

Feeling the Tree

When you are close enough, go up and touch the trunk of the tree. Peter Aziz recommends:

> *"... while keeping your hands in contact with the tree, begin to circle it slowly, in a clockwise direction. This is the direction of the Sun, Moon and stars, and will help the tree accept you as part of the natural order."*[7]

If there are two or more of you, you might want to link hands around the trunk and circle round like that.

Walk round the tree several times, becoming aware of what you are experiencing in each direction. Are roots and branches making it difficult for you to keep in touch with the trunk? Does the trunk feel different as you move around it? Are there points where you feel more comfortable than others?

Then, do what you feel you want to do. Hugging trees is one of those activities which is often characterised as indicating an unsound mind, or worse! But it is actually a very effective way of getting to know them and, in any case, there won't be anybody there to see you. So, go ahead and hug your tree, relaxing your body so that you feel moulded against the trunk itself. Climb it if you feel so inclined and are able to do so! There is nearly always an immediate positive response.

Explore the tree with all your senses, particularly feeling it - keeping your hands in contact with the bark as you do so. Does the tree give off a characteristic scent? What does its bark look like in detail? Are there any insects or other creatures which live in it?

After a time exploring in this way (and remember that you are in no hurry), you may be attracted to a particular part of the tree that feels right for you to sit down with your back against the trunk. It may be that you feel happy because you have instinctively found a place that 'fits' you when you sit down, or it could be that you feel happier sitting facing a particular direction or view out - somewhere that you feel secure and not so vulnerable or threatened. Seek out the special spot or spots around the tree and sit down. You may take some time to get comfortable, adjusting your body to accommodate the roots, branches and knobbly bits of trunk so that you feel you are in a position where you can relax fairly easily.

Attunement

When you have got comfortable, remind yourself that you are under no time limits, and that just being here with the tree is beneficial. You don't have to do anything, as Kiri Clay-Egerton reminds us:

> *"The one thing that still strikes me is the overpowering sensation of utter stillness and quietness which this old larch radiated over the whole area of the copse. In those days, because I lived close by, I used to come and go at will. This tree was, I found, so pure and calming that to me it became a sacred spot in a place of unlimited beauty.*
>
> *Its trunk was old, with deep ridged channels and prominent ribs in its bark. These were homes for many varieties of moss and lichens and their associated life-forms. Whether they performed any actual service for the tree was not a question which I ever asked or expected an answer to. This tree gave me an aura of beauty and yet utter solemnity while at the same time providing me with a backrest as I sat peacefully among its gnarled and twisted roots.*
>
> *I used to sit there with closed eyes, hearing and feeling the silence until slowly the tree began to talk to me in faint whispers, which slowly rose to a crescendo as its needles shivered and shook in the open air."*[26]

You may find that relaxing the body is a helpful thing to do, and it will mean that you will remain comfortable for longer, since your body will mould itself more easily to the tree roots, the ground between them, and the trunk.

There are various techniques for relaxation. I take a few consciously deep breaths, using the whole of the lungs and then visualise each part of the body relaxing. I often imagine unhooking or cutting tight elastic, or experiencing the tensions falling away into the earth.

The mind needs to be stilled as well. If you wish, you can close your eyes and imagine a still pool of water which can reflect perfectly. But you are actually in nature and don't have to imagine anything, so I find it easier, particularly if I am in a wood or near other trees, to watch them, and their twigs and leaves moving in the breeze, for they are rarely completely still.

Whatever method we use, in a few minutes a stiller sense creeps over us. This has been correlated with a change in the brain wave pattern, difficult to describe but easy to recognise in practice. Simon Lilly describes the process:

> "... you will find that after a little while in the presence of some trees you will, as it were, spontaneously feel "better". What could be happening here? We could suggest that the emotional disharmony or incoherent brainwave patterns of a disturbed person are influenced to become more coherent by the inherent harmony of the tree's structures (whether physical or subtle)."[63]

When you are in this state of deep relaxation, you sometimes 'come to' with a jolt if a leaf falls or a bird lands on a nearby branch, and the brain waves return to 'normal'. If this happens, just take it in your stride, settle down again and in a minute or two - perhaps more quickly with practice - you will be back in the deeply relaxed state.

Then, become aware of the tree - aim to merge with it, so that the energies flowing around your body flow out and into the tree, and the tree's energies flow into you, so that you are part of one system. It may help to envisage that you are "breathing with the tree". As Simon Lilly says:

> "... whether consciously or not, we have to interact with every other energy form in order to experience it and our perceptions are always modified by what is going on inside us. So generally, at least when one is in a state of a fairly positive dynamic balance, what one likes or finds attractive or beautiful is creating that sensation because it is in harmony with or creating greater harmony within our own energy systems."[63]

This is an idea which I expressed many years ago in a series of articles entitled "Landscape Energy and Experience"[46] and "Experiencing the Subtle Geography of the Earth"[47,48]. I suggested that our ability to find landscape attractive was related to the extent to which the life energies were able to flow freely through our bodies and not be blocked by muscular tensions.

This is a two-way process. As we relax, we can feel the energy flows strengthening within our own body, overcoming the blockages that we all have. Our body acts as a sort of 'receiver' so that, when we are in that state, we are more able to perceive the energy flows in the earth and other living beings, such as trees, and to interact with them. In other words, we open ourselves and allow the energy flows in the tree into our own body so that for a period of time we act almost as one system, as if, at some level, we have become one with the tree. Some have described this flow as an "energy balancing", for what is happening is that there is an interchange of energy taking place between ourselves and the tree. This can be a powerful healing process but it also allows more ready communication and identification with the tree to take place.

Initially, you may feel a surge of energy build up, as if your whole body were being flushed out with pure spring water, bright fire or crystal clear air. It may help, during this process, if you can visualise the tree's energy burning up or flushing out all that is negative within you, or taking it into itself and transforming it, or passing it down into the earth to neutralise it.

This may last some time, but will gradually become less intense as you enter a more stable state. Don't worry if you don't feel anything to start with, for things are probably happening anyway. Don't give up, for sitting under a tree in a relaxed state for even a few minutes is likely to prove of benefit to you. You can stay in this state for as long as you want to, particularly if you are wanting some healing for a part of your body that is in contact with the tree. This process is happening even if we are just standing near a tree or walking through the woods. It's just less intense and takes rather longer to achieve the same state.

You may, however, want some inspiration or knowledge, as I did in gathering material for this book. In my case I concentrated on the idea that I wanted to understand the character and personality inherent in, not just the tree that I was resting against, but all oaks, beeches, yews, or whatever. I wanted an insight into the essence of oak, as it were. After a while, I began to write and, whilst I don't claim them to be particularly inspired, what I wrote did help me to understand a bit more about quite a few of the trees that I approached. I found that, with pen and paper in hand, I could dip into and out of that special state of mind sufficient to be able to write down the thoughts and words that came to me.

In time one can write more fluently. As Steve Blamires has remarked: "... it will be up to you to learn to speak the language of the trees fluently"[15]. Chase and Pawlik have called this process "letting down the language barriers between you and the tree species" and remind us that learning to communicate with trees takes time and patience and that it is "our intent or the level of understanding that we seek that determines how we perceive the response"[23].

Experiencing the Tree Spirits

Tree energy can be experienced as pure energy/spirit or, as we have seen in the last chapter, it can manifest in folklore and mythology as living beings who take on form and can communicate with us. In Greek and later traditions they have been known as dryads.

Neither way of looking at and experiencing trees is wrong: it is very much a matter of what sort of person we are as an individual. We shouldn't worry if we can't see or feel anything at all, because things probably come to us in other ways, such as intuition and inspiration.

Anyway, some will find that they can see or experience tree spirits. I must admit that I am not much of a guide here because the most I have experienced is something out of the corner of my eye, on the very limits of vision. However, there are many who have seen, and we must follow what they say of their experiences in this respect. If you can see the Tree Spirits, then you will need no help from me. However, one thing which may help is to set up the circumstances which will best allow them to manifest and then see what happens.

They seem to use simulacra - that is, the quality which some natural things possess of looking like something else - particularly for our present purposes a face. We can see - indeed, imagine - faces in many things - the embers of a fire, a crumbling rockface or the foam of waves on the sea shore.[78] Trees are not immune from this: bark, leaves and roots all have potential for simulacra, particularly under certain light conditions, notably in the shade and at dusk and in moonlight, which allow the imagination to awaken and flourish and for an alternative reality to make an appearance. This is indeed imaginary, but that is one of the ways in which such beings manifest themselves - using natural forms and low light conditions as a stepping stone to full manifestation.

Don't worry if you can't see anything: there will be a part of you that can. The trick is to connect the part that can see with the part that can't. One quite effective way of doing this is to imagine what the tree spirits would be like if you could see them. Whilst it seems strange at first, it is actually an effective way of making those connections in the mind/brain stronger until you can actually see what you had imagined. Imagination, looked at in this way, is something to be welcomed and strengthened rather than suppressed.

It is important to use all the senses - you may not be able to see the tree spirits, but you may be able to feel or hear them. As Morgan Raven says, "You may begin to hear certain noises which herald the arrival of these beings or even faint whispers at the very limits of your hearing"[99].

We should also aim to have as few preconceptions as possible. The reason is fairly obvious - we are listening to the tree (with all our senses) and if our mind is full of ideas of what we might expect, then it will block, or at least distort, what is coming through to us. Paul Devereux called this approach 'being and seeing', where we bring no baggage with us - no cameras, or even notebooks. The only thing we are allowed is that rare commodity - an open mind.

It is really about living in the present, as John Fowles discovered when, whilst travelling through France, he came upon a Military Orchid, the first he had seen. He spent a long time making sure he had identified it correctly, measuring and photographing it, and working out exactly where he was, before he moved on. However, he continues:

"... five minutes after my wife had finally (other women are not the only form of adultery) torn me away, I suffered a strange feeling. I realized I had not actually seen the three plants in the little colony we had found. Despite all the identifying, measuring, photographing, I had managed to set the experience in a kind of present past, a having-looked, even as I was temporally and physically still looking. If I had had the courage, and my wife the patience, I would have asked her to turn and drive back, because I knew I had just fallen, in the stupidest possible way, into an ancient trap. It is not necessarily too little knowledge that causes ignorance; possessing too much, or wanting to gain too much, can produce the same result. ... We lack trust in the present, this moment, this actual seeing, because our culture tells us to trust only the reported back, the publicly framed, the edited, the thing set in the clearly artistic or the clearly scientific angle of perspective. One of the deepest lessons we have to learn is that nature, of its nature, resists this. It waits to be seen otherwise, in its individual presentness and from our individual presentness." [36]

This approach is very much in tune with the principles underlying Taoism and Zen Buddhism. It is also similar to the guidance given to those starting to paint or draw - to see the landscape as it is and not how we think (or worse still, know) it is.

In Tune with the Tree

You will know when you are in tune with the spirit of the tree, and you will then know how to develop that relationship. In all likelihood, it will simply be a matter of being there, experiencing the tree energy flowing through you, and knowing that you will benefit, in health and in wisdom, as a result.

Chase and Pawlik suggest formulating some general question, such as "What qualities of your being do I need to affirm?"[23], or you may have a specific problem or question which you want some guidance on. If so, formulate it in your mind, concentrate on it for a moment, and then let it go. An answer may come to you immediately, or it may come later, perhaps in a dream.

Just like people, individual trees differ - certainly the various types of trees differ. What I have written above applies generally, but you already know intuitively that each type of tree has its own character and "feel". The feeling that you get sitting against a yew may be very different from that obtained from an oak, for example. This can most definitely apply at the physical level - beech, for example, can be very comfortable to sit against, whereas holly, in my experience, always seems to be wanting you to get up and go after a relatively short period!

Breaking Contact

Stay in this state for as long as you wish, knowing that it will be of benefit to your whole being in so many ways. You will know the right time to come back again, but do it slowly, gently, returning to everyday reality. Steve Blamires suggests cushioning the blow by some ritual action which consciously breaks the contact with the tree:

> "this ... helps you to return to the faster moving, mundane world of people, thoughts, and actions. Be prepared; this can be quite a shock to the system after a deep session with a tree spirit"[15]

Stand up and stretch your legs. Touch or hug the tree and give thanks for the experience. This is largely a matter of genuinely feeling thanks, though it is quite appropriate to symbolise this by placing some token of respect by the tree, perhaps a small garland of flowers. Even some water will generally be greatly appreciated, or some practical work to help the tree.

Peter Aziz looks at it from a different angle when he says:

> *"What can you give a being that receives all it needs directly from the Goddess? If you need to give, question why you cannot receive freely and unconditionally. Or maybe it is your humility that needs questioning. Do you imagine that you can give on the same level as nature? We are all just children to the Goddess, we receive all we have from Her, and there is nothing we can give that is not already hers. So let the ego down, and accept your total dependence, and let yourself receive graciously and humbly. If you wish to give anything, give your love and devotion."*[7]

Ultimately, it is always a matter of what feels right to you as an individual. If you want to give some offering to the tree, then give it, but make sure it is appropriate.

Return - Building a Relationship

If we like someone, we usually want to see them again, and so it will be with trees. A deep experience with a tree will draw us closer to it and we will want to experience the tree at different seasons of the year, when it is expressing different sides of its character. And, if it is at all feasible, we will want to experience it at different times of day and month as well. The feeling on a warm spring morning will be very different from late twilight at the heart of summer, and different again under a Full Moon on a midwinter's night. Steve Blamires gives the deeper reason for doing this:

> *"This process will also reveal quite a bit about yourself, as you force yourself out in rain and snow, dark and*

cold, autumn and winter, as well as sun and warmth, daylight and brightness, and spring and summer. By getting to know the trees, and by building relationships with them, you are getting to know and build a relationship with your Self."[15]

Limitations and Opportunities

In this chapter, I have assumed that people have no difficulty in going out physically into the landscape to come into contact with a tree or trees. There are likely to be trees close to where most people live, and we must remember that one can contact the whole species by contacting one specimen. If you can possibly get to a tree to feel it, then do so. Those who are blind or visually impaired can gain exactly the same benefit as anyone else, as can those with other sensory deprivations.

However, there are some for whom it is impossible to visit a tree physically because of specific mobility problems, and these have to develop other ways of contacting trees. Primary here is what has variously been called pathworking, creative visualisation or guided meditation, where one might, for example, visualise moving through a wood, approaching a tree, and undertaking a similar exercise to that outlined in this chapter. This can be tremendously powerful and things can come through which are as real as if one were sitting against the trunk of the tree itself.

Dreams and out-of-the-body experiences can eventually come if one focuses on what one wants, and this can all be helped by holding a sample of the wood of the particular tree one wishes to contact whilst carrying out the pathworking or whatever. Leaves or pictures can also help, as can a small bottle of the relevant Tree Essence or Bach remedy.

What can we learn from trees?

Much that we learn from trees is not intellectual learning. Indeed, learning is probably not the right word to use, because a lot of the wisdom imparted by trees by-passes the mind altogether and makes a link directly with the body, mainly through the chakras. So, our heart and solar plexus, for example, can respond to the energies given out by the tree and can learn how to function more in accordance with their true nature.

We absorb from the trees that which we need and which we are lacking. In doing so, we take on at least some of their own qualities - the ability to see things from the long perspective and the wisdom that follows; to express the cycle of life, death and rebirth through our own lives; the realisation that we are not only separate beings but one with the rest of existence; being able to see the depths of meaning underlying things and recognising that life is far more than just this physical realm.

These great themes, and more, we can learn from trees - really learn them, with our heart, and our whole body, as well as with our mind. And as we shall see in the next chapter, each type of tree has its own quality and can illuminate a different facet of our nature.

Chapter 6

Explorations Into the Personality of Trees

"Lucy's eyes began to grow accustomed to the light, and she saw the trees that were nearest her more distinctly. A great longing for the old days when the trees could talk in Narnia came over her. She knew exactly how each of these trees would talk if only she could wake them, and what sort of human form it would put on. She looked at a silver birch: it would have a soft, showery voice and would look like a slender girl, with hair blown all about her face, and fond of dancing. She looked at the oak: he would be a wizened, but hearty old man with a frizzled beard and warts on his face and hands, and hair growing out of the warts. She looked at the beech under which she was standing. Ah! - she would be the best of all. She would be a gracious goddess, smooth and stately, the lady of the wood."

C.S. Lewis - *Prince Caspian*

Even the most unobservant of us are aware that not all trees are the same. We recognise an oak leaf and can distinguish it from that of a holly. And, even if we may not be able to spell out their distinguishing characteristics we can appreciate the difference between the mature beech tree and the hawthorn in the hedgerow. It is very much like the way we recognise a friend when we meet them in the street. We may not be able to describe their characteristics or draw their picture, but we recognise them just the same.

I try in this chapter to approach trees in the same way that I might a person - in other words, to give a feel for the personalities of several different species of tree, presenting a fairly brief word-picture that sums up their character. By "personality", I mean the character of the tree as it is experienced by people, setting out the main "themes" which make it up. This is surely only one part, perhaps a small part, of its total being, but, so long as we recognise this, we can do no other than focus on how the tree impinges on our own lives.

In gathering material for this chapter, I have tried to draw upon the whole realm of human interaction with trees, including personal experience, folklore, traditional uses and practices, references in literature and the character which emerges from studying the physical form and other qualities which the tree possesses.

On reading through various accounts of personal experiences with trees and on examining the folklore and alleged healing properties which attached to them, an interesting fact began to emerge. This was that some themes seemed to be common to a wide range of trees, so that I began to see them as characteristics of trees as a whole rather than of individual species. In other words, there were certain 'personality themes' which all, or at any rate many, trees possessed, and these are largely the same themes that emerged from examining the legends, folklore and mythology of trees.

Trees symbolise the 'cycle of life', from birth as a seed through to maturity and old age. But they also symbolise, often in vivid form, the continuation of that cycle into rebirth and immortality. Trees also function as doorways to the Otherworld, helping us to alter our consciousness so that we may more readily attune to those realms.

The link with the Otherworld implies an expansion of consciousness, which usually includes an inherent awareness of the way all things are part of the one whole. This linking of all things together lies at the root of what we might call 'the divinatory experience'. Trees have therefore naturally become the focus for divination, and the shapes and textures of roots, bark, branches and leaves, their movement in the wind, together with the atmosphere created by the scents and resins exuded by the trees and their associated plants, have all helped to create the circumstances which allow divination to occur.

To be within the presence of a tree - to touch it or in some cases identify even more closely with it - is, according to much folklore, to put yourself under its protection and to open oneself to its healing powers.

Trees have long been associated with fertility, mainly no doubt because of the way in which their yearly cycle is expressed. But they have also been seen as sources of knowledge about love and help with fertility problems, and this doubtless springs from their healing powers.

In writing the passage about each tree, I have drawn from a wide variety of sources, which are mentioned in the References section at the end of the book. Undoubtedly, however, the works of Helen McSkimming[72], Glennie Kindred[55] and Jacqueline Memory Paterson[91] stand out as examples so good that when I read each of them I was tempted to give up writing this book as they had said it all far more eloquently than I could myself.

And yet, I continued, and gradually perceived a distinctive path of my own through the wood. It seemed to me that, whilst the folklore and mythology surrounding the individual species, plus the healing remedies and recipes, were interesting in their own right, they were merely pointing the way towards some deeper and more integrated truth - what I have called the 'personality' of the tree. Thus I have tried to learn from the trees themselves, many of which have welcomed me as I sat with my back to their trunk, notebook in hand.

These descriptions of personality are a long way from being complete, either in terms of the number of trees covered, the qualities ascribed to each tree or the examples given. It has not been my intention to provide a complete catalogue of folklore, for example, attached to any particular tree. This has been done admirably by others, and I do not intend to emulate or repeat their work. I have limited myself to setting out what I consider to be just some of the main personality themes for each tree. I must point out that I have not been consistent here. I know some trees better than others and, to some extent, their personality has determined the form of the section devoted to them. I have tried to allow the wisdom present in the tree to unfold, for each tree has a lesson for our lives, if we can perceive it aright.

Partly for reasons of space and time, I have not included every tree. Apple and elm are notable by their absence, and sycamore, despite its strong pleas, has been excluded. Ivy, mistletoe, reed, bramble and gorse, though part of the old Celtic tradition, have been excluded on the justifiable grounds that they are not actually trees.

I tried out various different ways of arranging the sections into some logical sequence, but fell back eventually on alphabetical order, which actually has some justification, in that alder and birch are near the beginning, oak is in the middle and yew is firmly at the end, which is where it would be in any case. I don't know enough about how our alphabet developed in the order it did, or how the trees got their current names, but I detect some form of synchronicity or hidden unity flowing beneath the surface.

In Chapter 2 we saw that trees, like ourselves, have a subtle body as manifested in the aura, and flows of energy within and surrounding them. Whilst this principle seems common to all trees, each individual species seems to have its own energy pattern, which can be experienced by those who approach the tree in the right state of consciousness. It is also reflected in the physical form of the tree, as Sheldrake has indicated.

Ultimately, what I have tried to put across is the energy pattern of each tree, as revealed in their form and in people's responses to them. This is very much 'work in progress'. The energy flows and patterns in some trees seem very clear from the form of their branches, trunk, roots and leaves. Others I feel unsure about at this stage. This is not a fully worked-out system and I feel that it is important that I do not pretend that it is. The most that I can do is to note down my observations and leave others to complete (or even contradict) them.

In most books on the esoteric aspects of trees, an "astrological correspondence" is given. In other words, the character and nature of the particular species of tree in question is allocated to a particular planet - the implication being that the astrological qualities traditionally attributed to the planet in question are, if not identical, at least very close to those of the tree species concerned. I think it important to state that, certainly in my experience, they are not.

Trees have their own qualities - they are not representatives of pure planetary energies. The most that we can say is that some trees have very close correspondence with particular planetary energies (such as hawthorn with Venus during its may-blossom phase) and that others have qualities corresponding to several different planetary energies (such as birch, with its correspondences with the Moon, Venus and Saturn).

I have been most fortunate in having the services of Lesley Wilkinson to illustrate each of the trees which I have included. Her drawings are striking and I asked her to contribute a piece on her inspiration and work, which I give below:

"The fundamental inspiration precipitating this sequence of drawings sprang from meditations first entered into during the summer of ninety-six. I then took time out to visit sites where the different trees grew, sitting with them, touching them, quietly feeling the particular mood and emotion they engendered within me, listening to their individual voices. During these contemplations I also became increasingly and powerfully aware of the cyclical nature of all things, of the interplay of opposites, nature's multifarious things and of the unification and connectedness of all. The whole of Creation was seen as a ceaseless cyclic dance, endlessly making love to itself. I became interested in the ancient Ogham and the Tree Calendar finding that my own subjective feelings found much correlation to symbolic references pertaining to tree lore. From this wide basis I began to design pictorial equivalents of both my subjective feelings and objective study. Finally these actualised as illustrations for the twenty Ogham letters and their related trees. Thirteen of these drawings feature within the pages of this book along with an additional design, Beech not being part of the original sequence. The use of the human figure is utilised to depict the ever-changing face and mood of nature, as well as to emphasise the 'personality' of a particular tree. These figures, in male and female form, are also used, quite literally, as vehicle to translate and convey the vision Creation's love-dance."

ALDER - The Tree of Resistance
Alder is one of the pioneer trees. It has an affinity with water and is found along the banks of streams and other damp places. Indeed, it can grow half in water and half out. In low-lying ground it forms what is known as alder carr, which has

Alder

an undergrowth of rushes and reeds, and usually has willow and birch mixed in. Alders can also be found in mountain river valleys, along the edge of the streams or on the valley sides.

Whilst often just a big shrub in appearance, it can reach 150 feet in height. It usually develops a long straight trunk running up the whole tree, but its branches are very delicate, often bending over the nearby water.

Its leaves are sticky when young, to ward off moisture. Nuttall makes the further point that " ... *at the beginning of its life its very existence seems to hang on the proximity of water; for, when the seeds fall ripe from the parent tree and are seeking a lodgment, they are not furnished with wings or parachutes for flight, as are those of the sycamore or the poplar; but they are provided with airtight cavities inside their walls, so that they will float unharmed along the surface of stream or lake; a coat of oil, too, keeps them taut and dry, however long they swim*"[89].

Whilst alder has an affinity with water, its essential quality is that it can resist and withstand water. It has a quiet, somewhat hidden, strength, which is reflected in its physical, medicinal and magical uses and in the folklore and legend which has accumulated round it.

Alder has stability and solidity. It gives strength under prolonged pressure. It also acts as a shield and protection against corruptive powers. Characteristic of these qualities is the use to which alder has traditionally been put - to form the piles which are sunk into marsh or fen to act as the foundation for a house. Indeed, a major quality of alder is that of unobtrusive service and quiet resistance, doing a thing without a lot of fuss and ostentation.

The other elemental link which alder has is to fire. It burns badly but, in consequence, makes very good charcoal. In fact, alder can be seen as a tree of fire for, being a pioneer tree, it can gradually enable the land to emerge from the water. Helen

McSkimming has likened it to "the fire of will slowly coming out from the darkness of origin"[72]. Symbolic of this is the way in which, when cut, the white wood turns red as though bleeding.

Indeed, the essence of the fire aspect to the alder is that it will help with rebirth and the withstanding and coming through the storms of strong emotions.

ASH - The Tree of Strength

Ash is one of the largest and most prominent of trees, often planted near human settlement and found in oak and beech woods.

Nuttall has described its form:

> "As the Ash stands in its full beauty of summertide it is a goodly sight. The curving of its branches, which tend to droop and then rise at the tips, and a certain quality of airiness in its foliage due to the subdividing of its leaves, have caused it to be called the 'Venus of the Forest'."[89]

Ash wood is straight and strong and John Michell has pointed out that "The STR sound is strongly connected with straightness and strictness of conduct"[79]. It has long been used for staffs, spear shafts, broom handles and the like.

Ash can give us inner qualities of strength. It is not sentimental nor indulgent, but it will help us if our desire is for self-control in the various aspects of our life. It strengthens our sense of duty and is closely correlated with the planet Saturn.

Ash

Ash will give backing, is reliable and will be there when needed. It provides solid and long-lasting strength which enables the individual to go out and achieve. It truly provides en-courage-ment, but won't do anything for you: it expects you to do as much as you can to help yourself.

Ash is also practical - it will help us to find ways in which we can best express in our everyday lives the insights we have obtained in the higher realms. Its role as the broomstick is a practical demonstration of this, as is its frequent use as the personal and ritual stang.

BEECH - The Queen of the Woods

Beech trees have been very special to me for as long as I can remember. If I was depressed or needed some sort of perspective on my life I knew that a grove of mature beech trees would provide what I needed.

And yet beech has often been regarded as a 'second class citizen', based, I think, on Julius Caesar's statement that there were no beech in Britain. He was wrong, as pollen analysis has now proved, but the absence of beech from Robert Graves' Tree Calendar, for example, has led many modern pagans to ignore or undervalue the tree.

Indeed, it was described to me as "the secret one", when I revealed that I intended to include beech in my book (and what more appropriate since the words 'beech' and 'book' have the same roots) with the implication, which I would fully endorse, that the reason it is not included in most pagan tree literature is that it is too special, too sacred, too important.

Beech trees are common in most places, but they grow best on the chalk - from Dorset up to the Yorkshire Wolds - with the heartland being the Chiltern Hills where, from Burnham Beeches to Ashridge, are some of the greatest stands of beech

Beech

in the country. Beeches are shady trees: they don't let through much sunlight. So there's very little plant life growing beneath them, just the characteristic carpet of fallen brown beech leaves, creating what Nuttall calls "haunts of deep mystery".

The roots of the beech are shallow, which tends to make it vulnerable to heavy winds, and many were blown over in the 1987 hurricane, including those at Chanctonbury Ring on the Sussex Downs. Because of their proximity to the surface, the roots are highly visible and form a prominent feature in the localised landscape. Tennyson referred to the 'serpent-rooted beech' and their root pattern has also been likened to a labyrinth.

Where beeches grow close together, in a copse or beechwood, their trunks will grow up without lower branches, to a height of 60 feet or more. This has frequently been likened to the columned aisle of a Gothic cathedral, emphasised by the smooth grey trunks. Indded, this quality is often so striking that it seems clear that a beech grove must have been the prime inspiration for that style of architecture.

The solitary beech is different. The bark is particularly sensitive to light, and so, in addition to the effect of the leaves, which we have already noted, the tree will keep its lower branches, thus forming the characteristic protective and all-encompassing shape that clearly says "You are here. You need go no further."

Beech is, as I have mentioned, a very special tree to me and there are many individual beeches, from Devon to Northumberland, that I have sat against and felt the warmth flow within me. Most of the sites that I frequent to perform the seasonal rituals have beech trees as their focus.

There is something special about beech - it is said to be the tree that is closest to humans and therefore the easiest to communicate with. The presence of a beech seems to make a place special - makes it somewhere in its own right, and I feel that people were often led to plant beeches at places that they felt were especially significant in some way.

The most nearly human of the trees

Beech has one of the smoothest of all barks, and this, coupled with the rounded and sinuous shapes frequently made by its trunk, roots and lower branches, makes us think of the human body.

Perhaps more than any other tree, it seems to want to be touched. Here are no prickles or rough bark, but something very like our own skin. Certainly in my experience beech is by far the most comfortable tree to sit against. The shape of one's back and of the beech trunk somehow seem made for each other, and it therefore seems possible to get closer to a beech tree, both physically and spiritually, than to any other.

This tactile and sensuous quality including the smoothness of the bark, seems to attract lovers, perhaps by sympathetic magic, as a place to meet - a 'trysting tree' - and as somewhere to carve their initials. We have already noted how the sensuous quality of the beech seems to have long been an attraction, and this is, of course, in no way unusual, in that modern pagans do all this - hugging and kissing trees, lying in their shadow and offering them libations of wine - and the beech still draws us to it to do these things.

Comfort and Warmth

Beech is comforting. It is the tree that one would choose to shelter under and to sleep against at night, as we have already seen in the passage from "*The Wind in the Willows*" in Chapter 4 and as did Wat Brand in Brian Bates' "*The Way of Wyrd*":

"After a time an early owl hooted in the forest below and thunderclouds rolled darkly across the sky. I decided to seek the shelter of the forest. Crossing myself, I rose quickly to my feet, scooped up my shoulder-bag and cloak and climbed down the hill, picking my steps carefully at first, then stumbling and sliding on my backside. Eventually I stepped through thinly spaced beeches which skirted the forest like silent sentries. Woodland shadows reached out to envelop me and it was too dark to follow animal paths; I had to work my way carefully through the trees, wading through thick undergrowth of golden fern and clinging brambles until, without warning, I emerged into a small clearing completely canopied by one gigantic beech tree. From the base of the beech two immense roots like dragon's claws rambled half-way across the open space. Working quickly in the gathering gloom, I heaped dry leaf-litter into the space between the roots to form a mattress. The shadows melted into darkness."[10]

This is a good description of the way in which the circular spread of the branches, reaching out to the ground, make an enclosure. Little will grow here, and the carpet of beech leaves is a characteristic form.

Beech has been called "The Mother of Forests" and it certainly acts like a mother, soothing any irritation, helping understanding and then cheering and inspiring confidence and even joy. It brings us back to the present, sustaining us and helping our spirit to manifest effectively in the physical plane.

Susan Lavender and Anna Franklin say:

"Beech is a useful plant for anyone who feels they may be getting too dogmatic or narrow minded about their beliefs. The beech will help free the mind from its constrictions and to reconnect with the higher purpose."[59]

This comfort and warmth leads naturally to a more tolerant and understanding view of the world. This is emphasised by the Bach Flower Remedy, which is appropriate for "those who feel the need to see more good and beauty in all that surrounds them."[8] This, in turn, encourages a more adventurous view of life, where increasing self-confidence results in creative action.

BIRCH - The Lady of the Wood

The quality of the birch is delicate and aethereal, inhabiting the space between this world and the world of faery. It purifies, and then encourages rebirth and new growth, fertility and love to prosper. The birch possesses great strength and hardiness and sacrifices its own life for the good of the whole.

Birch is a pioneer tree, being one of the first to recolonise after the retreat of the ice caps. It is still the pioneer and its seeds can carpet an area with thousands of small seedlings in only a few months. I know abandoned railway marshalling yards where self-seeded birch trees, left to their own devices, have made quite a respectable wood in only a few years.

Nuttall, quoting from Lowell (1819-1891) describes the birch vividly:

> "A gleaming silver trunk, foliage dripping 'like the tresses of a Dryad, tiny leaves that palpitate for ever,' softening the outline in a tender green mist and all fused in the alchemy of pale spring sunshine, make up a sight than which there is none more beautiful in the whole tree world."[89]

Grace and Delicacy

The birch is one of the most beautiful of trees, being light and delicate in appearance and this is a key to one aspect of its

Birch

character. It is flowing and flexible. Nuttall shows how the delicacy is arrived at:

> "A study of Birch branching in winter days shows that the trunk runs as a definite, albeit tapering, column to the very tip of the tree, and that the branches that it gives off are considerably slighter and darker. From these branches droop still slighter twigs whose ultimate ramifications are almost thread-like."[89]

This provides strength - the strength that comes through suppleness and stretching. It is good for our spine and helps to give us tolerance and flexibility.

With the wind allowing its leaves to flutter, it looks as if it is dancing and, in its turn, it makes us dance and think quickly, sing and move lightly. Dorothy Maclean received something on this from the Birch Deva:

> "How could our leaves flutter without the wind, how could our bark shine white without the light, how would we stand upright without the earth to feed and hold us, how would we be watered without the cloud and the sun to make the cloud?
>
> We exult in what we are, for so it is. We rejoice in any consciousness that appreciates what we are, that appreciates the fineness, precision and delicacy, the power and patience which culminate in a birch tree. We stand in our positions here and, as we stand, we spread that which we have to contribute for all to see."[70]

Birch has a fragrant aroma after rain has fallen and, because of its resinous content, the bark also has an attractive scent when burnt.

The Most Aethereal of Trees

Nuttall's description of the delicacy of the birch, Coleridge's "Lady of the Wood", is only one aspect, that which is most obviously seen.

But the birch is also the most aethereal of trees, the one nearest to the land of faery - the Otherworld - and hovers on that point that is neither and both - that "boundary between the worlds" - and we shall note other connections between the birch and boundaries later.

This aethereal quality is strongest in moonlight, when the silver rays of the Full Moon are reflected off the silver bark of the birch's trunk to create a magical space to move silently through, where each tree is a manifestation of the Goddess of the Woods, watching, enchanting and enfolding. Nuttall reminds us of a magical moment:

> "A group of well-grown Birch trees, lighted by a winter sunset, will give a remarkable scenic phenomenon, for their fringe-like multitude of branchlets and their gleaming trunks together produce the effect of a purplish haze cut through with vertical lines of silver."[89]

Symbol of Purification

Springing from its delicacy and aethereal nature, birch can act as a purifier, refining us and, just as it sheds its bark, so it can release old patterns of life that are negative or no longer appropriate. This can work at a deep level as this aethereal and spiritual nature of the birch seeps into us as we stand, sit or lie in the midst of a birch wood, and increases our ability to experience peace and beauty. It seems as if the light filtering through the branches and leaves can in itself help to purify.

Lavender and Franklin have expressed it thus:

"Magically, the vibration of the birch is the power of ... leaving behind the winter and negativity, cleaning and purification in preparation for the summer ... The white trunk of the birch represents the shining light of purity and freshness and may be used as a totem to rid yourself of things that must be left behind."[59]

This purification can have more physical manifestations, too, since birch twigs are used to beat the skin following a sauna, and until recently used on the Isle of Man as a traditional form of punishment. The idea behind this was that the birch would purify and drive evil from the body.

Being the first tree to appear, birch is concerned with making its own boundaries. It has been used instinctively to make things connected with boundaries, such as beating the bounds of a parish, birching for those who transgress the boundaries of the law, and the use of the broomstick to make the threshold.

Robert Graves points out that traditionally the birch was used for ceremonial flagellation coupled with the ingestion of the Fly agaric which induces shamanic visions and which is found growing beneath birch trees.[42]

The besom - the traditional broomstick made from an ash handle, birch twigs and bound in willow - is now almost the symbol for the witch. In former days, however, when it was dangerous to be caught in possession of magical implements, it was the handle itself which was the magical staff or wand, often carved in a phallic shape, which was then disguised by being hidden by the twigs. Thus the broom became associated with sex and fertility, and jumping across the besom was long used as a form of marriage. The broom, however, has a magical function in itself, with the act of sweeping being symbolic of driving out the spirits of the old year, in the Celtic tradition - another example of the birch acting as a boundary marker between one year and the next.

The New Start - Inception

Purification is really only one side of the equation. Birch is also very much about the new start, providing a very pure and delicate environment allowing the growth of new ideas and attitudes. Symbolic of this, it is the earliest forest tree (excluding the elder) to put out new leaves.

Symbol of Springtime and Rebirth

Spring was celebrated by the collection of birch sap, which was made into wine. This was considered to release the spirit of the tree to give its power to the strengthening sun.

This link with new life and fertility is emphasised by the traditional use of birch for maypoles, which were, in fact, originally, living trees. The Beltane fires were lit with birch twigs, and the wild celebrations at that time of year frequently took place in birchwoods.

The birch has long been poetically associated with love. The giving of a birch wreath was a token of love and a lover's bower was often located beneath a birch tree.

Strength and Hardiness

Birch is a hardy tree, being capable of resisting frost when young, which is one of the reasons it can be found further north than any other tree. It can also grow on the poorest soil and high up on mountains, and it seems as if its association with fungi enables it to obtain any available nourishment very efficiently.

Self-sacrifice

Whilst birch does not take much from its environment it gives a lot in terms of what it is. Birch is pure and, in performing its pioneer function, is ultimately called upon to sacrifice itself. It

Blackthorn

is a short-lived tree in any case, but what is happening is that other, longer-lived, trees such as oak are growing up in the shade and protection which birch offers. The rotting birch leaves enrich the soil and provide a favourable environment for the seedlings of larger trees like oak and beech. These out-grow the birch, depriving it of the light that allows it future growth, eventually killing it. This is like the hero who must die to make way for those who are younger and stronger.

BLACKTHORN - Stillness and Severity

Blackthorn rarely grows into the shape of a tree and naturally forms an impenetrable thorny thicket up to 15 feet high. Because of these qualities it is frequently used in hedging, along with hawthorn.

It has angular branches with thorns and dark knobbly twigs and is one of the earliest flowering shrubs. From early March, its white blossom can frequently be seen, forming what has been described as a mist against the dark wood.

Clarity and Stillness

The thorns and the white flowers in the clear cold air of early spring all go to promote the clarity of stilled thoughts, the ability to think unemotionally about what the right course of action is. It has the stillness of deep waters, and in attuning to it we can become aware of the cycle of all things and our place within it.

Blackthorn enables us to think positively but realistically - to see ourselves as we are, though Jacqueline Memory Paterson issues a warning:

> "... such is the purgative nature of the blackthorn and its winter fruit that its action can be harsh and unrelenting as it pushes us closer to karmic issues. For those who

need a gentler process, the spring blackthorn with its
massed white blossoms provides a lighter cleansing ..."[91]

Seriousness and Severity

Blackthorn is, however, serious and severe and it can help us when we are determined to change ourselves or the circumstances in which we find ourselves.

Helen McSkimming puts it clearly:

> *"The Blackthorn is often associated with the cold, winter winds from the North. Both are seen as being potentially destructive and conveyers of things hidden. Like the Hag, they bring about transformation and change, taking away so that new formations can take place."[72]*

This is the so-called "Blackthorn Winter" - the cold spell, with north-easterly winds, which seem to encourage the blossom to appear.

Power

But blackthorn is also a tree of strong and severe power. It is used as a magical wand, stang or staff which can summon the Wild Hunt and act as a 'blasting rod' for cursing. This is a serious matter, as Lavender and Franklin warn us:

> *"Any weapon or staff made from blackthorn must be used with great care, for strength and power without compassion and wisdom can just as easily destroy the wielder as the target. The energy of the sloe is a difficult one to assimilate and can trap the unwary."[59]*

Evan John Jones continues this theme:

"As it is a wood of ill-omen, the only use of the blackthorn stang is in the solemn rite of a formal cursing. In this guise, it is the representative of the Two-Faced God. From the same stem comes the power that can be used for both good and evil; a face which should be rarely invoked or worked."[53]

The Unapproachable Barrier

The severity and power of blackthorn combine to create an impenetrable barrier, a protection against attack. Blackthorn thickets helped to keep the Romans out of Anglesey, thus retaining it as a Druidic stronghold. It is also said that blackthorn thickets are good psychic barriers, impregnable against all except love, and that this is the origin of the 'Sleeping Beauty' legend.

ELDER - The Mother

Elder is familiar to most of us, with its characteristic scent and with its creamy white flower-heads, which flourish in June, and its deep red Autumn berries making it a prominent feature of the landscape during these periods.

Elder loves to grow in wild corners of land in both countryside and town. It thrives on wasteland at the edges of human habitation, particularly on the chalk, though it will grow on very poor soils. It is a feature of small, often forgotten, woods, or on the edges of larger ones. Like hawthorn, it is often found growing above springs or holy wells.

It rarely exceeds 30 feet in height, often being considered more of a bush than a tree. Nuttall describes its form and growth:

"It is then, at the most, about 30 feet high, a curious tree in habit and growth, its very plan of life militating against it becoming a tree of any size. At the outset

Elder

several stems will often put in an appearance at the base. Each grows upright for a time, then droops over, and the bud that arises on the top of the curve is the one that will carry on, for a while, the upward growth. Then this shoot droops in turn, and the bud on the top of its curve gives an erect, strong substitute. Thus the main trunk of the elder is not built up in a straightforward fashion as is, say, the oak, but is a patchwork of the bases of many drooping shoots. It is obvious that this mode of growth cannot make for the stature of a giant, or for elegance, or indeed for anything else but irregularity and peculiarity."[89]

Because of this habit, its main trunk is not usually tall but, like the hawthorn, it looks old before its time, being rough and deeply furrowed, though its branches are smoother and its newest shoots green.

The Elder Mother

Above all, the elder symbolises the female cycle of maiden, mother and crone, the leaves, flowers and fruit representing these three phases of the Goddess cycle.

There were strong folk beliefs, particularly in Britain and Scandinavia, that the Elder Mother dwelt within the tree. In Denmark, for example, the Goddess Hulda, mother of the elves, was thought to live amongst its roots. Indeed, many of the folk names ascribed to it such as Holda, Hulda, Hilda, Helen, Elen and Ellern, are Goddess names.

The Elder Mother could work magic over the surrounding area and those who entered it. It was seen as a powerful witch tree as a result - one that avenged any injury to it. The consequence of this is that it was considered unlucky to cut the tree without asking permission of the Elder Mother. The wood was, in any case, not favoured for furniture and particularly not for cradles as it was thought that the fairies would come and take any baby which was laid in such a one.

The Hag and Crone

During the winter, the Elder represents the Crone and is particularly sacred to Hecate, guardian of the crossroads, keeper of the doors between the worlds. At such a season, an elder growing at a crossroads was traditionally considered to be particularly powerful.

In terms of character, the presence of maiden, mother and crone can certainly be felt, particularly that of the wise mother, encouraging and chastising in turn. Sitting under an elder can often show you clearly where your duty and commitment lie, making you aware of your responsibilities and encouraging you to do what is right and honourable.

The Elder Mother acts as a guardian and protector of an area. Often this can be embodied in a tree sited over a spring, which is a position of great power. This protective role caused many elders to be planted close to houses to guard the inhabitants against evil influences.

The Witch Tree and the Fairy Tree - Seeing Things in a Magical Way

The power to see beneath the surface of things - to see magically - is bestowed by the Elder, and its sap was traditionally used to anoint the eyes to encourage clairvoyance. Its association with both witches and fairies thus becomes clear: witches can see magically and fairies can be seen only by magical means. Perhaps the practice of frequenting elder trees on the part of witches, who then quietly slipped away into the dark, led to tales that witches were able to transform themselves into Elder trees to escape detection.

Elder is also favoured by the fairies, or sidhe. Helen McSkimming recounts that:

> *"In the days when it was still considered important to be on amicable terms with the Sidhe, the people always planted an Elder by their dwelling place and its care was entrusted to one person within each generation of the family to ensure that it was never neglected, so incurring the wrath of the Sidhe."*[72]

This gives another reason for the presence of elder near human habitation - one now almost completely forgotten.

It is said that you should never sleep beneath an Elder tree, because the fairies would carry you off, an indication, perhaps, of the power of the elder to assist in changes in consciousness, and thus a powerful tree to meditate under. Elder is strongly associated with the Otherworld. It is seen as the guardian of the gateways between the worlds, which can be found beneath the tree.

The Right Ordering of Things - Continuity through the Seasons

All trees remind us of the cycle of the year and of our own cycle of birth, death and rebirth, but the elder is one that is particularly associated, not just with regeneration and the eternal present, but with that fixed centre around which all revolves - the Elder Mother that we can come back to - stern but approachable. She shows us that we all have a place in the scheme of things - that we must value ourselves but not become egotistical, or we will be reprimanded.

Elder is particularly a tree of regeneration, because damaged branches can be replaced by new shoots from the central trunk, and indeed many parts of the tree will root and re-grow rapidly.

The Image of the Elder

Elder has a poor reputation and, in the words of Richard Mabey, is "... now widely regarded as little more than a jumped-up weed, a ragamuffin haunter of dung-heaps and drains."[69]

This seems to be largely a reaction because of its association with witchcraft, the Crone and death, which degenerated, under Christian influence, into an association with evil. Certainly it became considered an unlucky tree.

A Healing Tree

On the positive side, however, elder has been called "the medicine chest of the country" and nearly all its parts have been used for healing purposes.

HAWTHORN - The Tree of Wild Beauty

Hawthorn can grow up to 50 feet tall, but usually it is more like a large shrub. It is a pioneer tree and began to spread with the Neolithic forest clearances. Wilkinson says that on neglected land it can form continuous scrub, often growing up into "gloomy woods in which nothing else can grow". It is still seen today on wasteland and on the edges of woods and is a sign of human habitation. It can be very striking as a lone tree in the middle of a field.

Nuttall describes the form of the tree well:

> " ... under winter skies its crown of bare branches stands out dense and matted-looking, while more often than not it is broader than high. Its trunk is gnarled, the bark thick and scored by furrows along its length, so that the whole tree has a venerable and aged appearance"[89].

Hawthorn

Hawthorns can live for over 400 years, but the tree often appears older than it is, because the trunk is fluted and gnarled, often bearing a likeness, according to Paterson, to twisted old rope.

> *The buds, which appear early in the year, go on to develop into either leaves, thorns or flowers. The flowers are the most magnificent, transforming the tree during the month of May (which gives the tree one of its alternative names) into a mass of white flower-heads, which Milton described as moonlight-coloured. Nuttall sums up the feeling of many when he says that: "... the Hawthorn has always stood as an integral part of that supreme ideal, the English countryside in springtime, when earth is a fairyland and life a joy."*[89]

Hawthorn at its time of flowering is almost pure Venus - to do with attraction, love and sex, with intimacy and joy, with fertility and creation. Hawthorn opens up our power to love - finds the love hidden within, perhaps deep within, and brings it to the surface. Weighed down with its flower-heads, hawthorn attracts. It is said that the scent of the flowers reminds some men of the scent of female sexuality, and McSkimming has called hawthorn "representative of the wild, intuitive feminine principle". The blossom has an aphrodisiac effect and has been used as a powerful sexual attractant at May festivities. The fully mature hawthorn seems overflowing with joy.

This, in its positive and negative aspects, seems to be the reason why it was often considered unlucky to bring the may blossom indoors. From the positive point of view, it represented Nature: it was the time of year for celebrating outside and may blossom looks far better on the tree. On the negative side, it represented the wild, unrestrained quality of Nature, opening doorways to the Otherworld, something which many people were frightened of and wanted to escape from. It Celtic name, 'Uath', means 'frightful'. By bringing may blossom into the house they were reminded, perhaps unwelcomely, that there was another approach to things - a reminder, in short, of the Old Religion.

Fertility and creation spring naturally from this approach, and hawthorn seems to epitomise the act of creation - a demonstration of change over time, of things coming to fruition; and the drawing of energy from the Earth and the sky, resulting in the flowering of creation.

Hawthorn is also about the twin principles of the creation of space and protection. The trunk and roots are a visible manifestation of the flows of energy at the surface of the Earth, creating form out of pure energy, creating the sense of location and local space - the feeling that this tree with this trunk is the most important in the world and that it creates a sense of here-ness in both space and time - a sense of place and a sense of history. Its wide use in hedging is symbolic of this sense of creation of space. Hawthorn trees were also used to define the 'haw' or magical enclosure.

One reason it was used so often for hedges was that it formed a good impenetrable barrier. Linked with this, hawthorn naturally forms a protective barrier, and there is space beneath the spreading branches (and they are spreading, if you get underneath) to shelter and gain protection from lightning, as well as to gain invisibility, for a hawthorn hedge also provides good psychic protection.

HAZEL - The Poet's Tree

The hazel is rarely a tree on its own - one that is noticed in its own right. Rather, it is generally just a big bush, growing not much more than 20 feet in height, forming undergrowth, in pine, oak and mixed woods, although there are occasional woods of pure hazel, particularly in upland valleys. It prefers damp conditions but is actually very adaptable.

Hazel

Hazel flowers long before any other tree, as Nuttall recounts:

"In blustering gales and gusty sleet the Old Year had given place to the New, winter was in its most dreary aspect, and the branches of the trees stood out in sheer bareness. Suddenly, one spot by the copse's side arrested attention, for there, on what was little better than a shrub, the nakedness of the branches was decked by dancing tassels of gold, and into the sodden, rain-swept landscape there came a hint of gaiety, a whisper of spring. It was just a group of two or three Hazel trees, first of all Nature to bring the welcome of flowers to the new-born year."[89]

Hazel tends to have no central trunk, and the historical coppicing of the tree has intensified this habit. The resultant stems are reddish-brown in colour. The correlation with Mercury which is often given to Hazel is absolutely fitting, for there is quickness of energy which encourages thought and the learning of skills, as Paterson remarks:

"The atmosphere around a hazel tree is easily recognizable, for it is quick-moving and mercurial, like silvery fish. In south-west Britain country people say that 'silver snakes' surround the hazel's roots, which illustrates the swiftness of its energies."[91]

Hazel is about craft and crafts, about knowing how to do something without having to learn it or think about it, and therefore about inspiration. It is about the knowledge that comes with wisdom and the wisdom that comes with knowledge.

When we think of the hazel, we think of nuts. The nut was considered capable of encapsulating knowledge and wisdom, as Graves points out:

"The nut in Celtic legend is always an emblem of concentrated wisdom: something sweet, compact and sustaining enclosed in a small hard shell - as we say: 'this is the matter in a nut-shell'."[42]

He goes on to say:

"The Rennes Dinnshenchas, an important early Irish topographical treatise, describes a beautiful fountain called Connla's Well, near Tipperary, over which hung the nine hazels of poetic art which produced flowers and fruit (i.e. beauty and wisdom) simultaneously. As the nuts dropped into the well they fed the salmon swimming in it, and whatever number of nuts any of them swallowed, so many bright spots appeared on its body. All the knowledge of the arts and sciences was bound up with the eating of these nuts ..."[42]

Hazel is the tree that is closest to the human mind and it can therefore teach most readily. It does this by creating the atmosphere of learning - of drawing out from the mind what is already there, the true meaning of education being "to draw out", and of opening the mind to new concepts so that it is more ready to accept them. It will help you to become aware of and to trust your intuitive faculties and to dissolve any creative blocks which may have developed.

Just being in the presence of hazel is beneficial, according to Paterson:

"The greatest healing provided by hazel is found within its atmosphere. Being near hazel trees or meditating upon a piece of hazel brings the spirit alive and allows us to quickly cast off the old and move on to the new. Hazel's atmosphere exudes exhilaration and inspiration. ... It was called the 'poet's tree', for in the minds of the ancients it had great associations with faerie lore and supposedly allowed entrance into such realms."[91]

This focus on knowledge, wisdom and intuition means that it is an important tree for divination. The dowsing rod was, traditionally, a forked hazel twig, which was used to find water. Hazel was used partly because of its flexibility but also, I suspect, because of its qualities, enabling a contact with the human mind to be more easily made - a power link between humans and trees.

This power can be very real, as Arthur Ransome vividly describes in *"Pigeon Post"*:

> *"And at that moment Titty almost stumbled. ... It couldn't be the stick itself pressing against the soft flesh at the base of her thumbs. She pulled herself together. Silly to be startled like that. And anyhow nothing could have happened. Why, Dick himself had said that nothing could. ...Titty's eyes were swimming. She saw the ground of the yard at her feet through a mist. Something queer was happening that she could neither help nor hinder. The stick was more than a bit of wood in her hands. It was coming alive. If only she could drop it, and be free from it. ... Suddenly, a yard or so from the pump, there could be doubt no longer. The ends of the stick were lifting her thumbs. She fought against them, trying as hard as she could to hold them still. But the fork of the stick was dipping, dipping. Nothing could stop it. Her hands turned in spite of her. "Titty! Titty!" They were all talking to her at once. The next moment the stick had twisted clean out of her hands. It lay on the ground, just a forked hazel twig with the green showing through the bark where Nancy's knife had trimmed it. Titty, the dowser, startled more than she could bear, and shaking with sobs, had bolted up into the wood."*[98]

Because of its use for divination, hazel is often the chosen wood for a magic wand. The Druids, for example, frequently had wands of hazel to help give them poetic inspiration.

I said at the beginning of this section that hazel is rarely noticed in its own right. It is the tree that goes unnoticed, and this quality is used to good effect in that it can deflect and can preserve itself by becoming invisible. This quality can be acquired by the human, as Graves recounts:

> *"... in the Book of St. Albans (1496 edition) a recipe is given for making oneself as invisible as if one had eaten fern-seed, merely by carrying a hazel-rod, a fathom and a half long with a green hazel-twig inserted in it."*[42]

Hazel leaves contain the power of invisibility, as we have seen above, but also the power of intuition and inspiration in a very particular way. A sprig of hazel, with the leaves attached, can be as powerful a learning tool and inspirer as, for example, the Qabalah. At the right time, it can be a highly significant gift, conveying with it many qualities that the individual can internalise.

HOLLY - The Survivor

Holly is always vital and alive. One of the four native evergreens, it symbolises the principle of the "ever-green" - that which is always actively synthesising energy from the light - with the principle of focused and concentrated energy - manifested in its characteristic leaf prickles.

Holly was part of the great forests which sprung up after the last ice age. It was, and still is, found as a relatively low-growing shrub in woods of oak and beech, its size being limited because of its shady position. With the clearance of the forest for agricultural and other reasons, it started to grow in greater size and abundance.

It has been used for, and in, hedges because it forms an impenetrable barrier. It was often left untrimmed because it was felt to be particularly holy and, where it is in good light, a

Holly

holly tree can grow up to 40 feet in height. The holly is slow-growing, and a thick trunk is often the sign of a particularly old tree. Branches grow out from the central trunk all the way up, but it is often only the leaves lower than about 12 feet from the ground that have prickles, because these are the ones that are most vulnerable to browsing animals. The grey bark is fine and smooth and has been described as being somewhat silvery.

The male and female flowers are usually on separate trees. They come out in May or June. The female flower becomes the holly berry, but this can only happen if there is a male tree nearby.

Vitality

The life-energy is perhaps more apparent in the holly than in any other tree. Certainly it is busier, being kept moving and focused by the points on the holly's leaves, which act rather like the points on an ioniser. All the energy is concentrated at one point, resulting in its moving round at an incredible speed.

Indeed, if you want to see tree energy at work, start with the holly. It has an aura, but it consists of energy moving rapidly round. Its generally attributed planetary correspondence of Mercury is, for once, entirely appropriate.

In ancient tradition, the Holly King ruled the waning half of the year, from Midsummer to Midwinter. The culmination of his reign, at the Winter Solstice, is the time when the holly is at its most magnificent, with the vivid colour contrast between the green leaves and red berries. Its life-energy, in contrast with many other trees, is most apparent at this time, and it has long been used as a seasonal decoration.

Paterson draws our attention to the way in which, on a cloudless day, the shiny leaves actually seem to reflect the blue of the sky to contribute to the appearance of the aura itself. She sees the holly as symbolising "the energies of life in the midst of death" and Glennie Kindred describes it as "a powerful symbol of potent life energy".

Defensive Survival

Linked to, and as a development of, the principle of life in death is the theme of survival. Holly will survive even the destructive power of those whose aim is to ravage the plant by hacking off all the branches within reach to sell the sprigs of leaves and berries for excessive profit at Christmas time, as seems to happen around all large centres of population.

But holly is a survivor. Indeed, it survives better than any other tree. It can grow again and can renew itself from the most terrible depredations, if it is left alone and forgotten about. Its own inner strength will win through and this inner strength springs ultimately from its abundant life force. This is, of course, symbolised by its prickles. It seems a self-contained tree, providing comfort and protection. It lifts the spirits and kindles hope for the rebirth of the year.

Trees can give us what we lack and they can also help us to face themes in our own lives. So, the holly will bring us face to face with issues to do with protection, defence and survival. We need to balance these in our own lives, avoiding on the one hand being too vulnerable to outside forces and on the other being so defensive that we ultimately withdraw from any human contact. The Bach remedy for Holly, for example, is described as being "for those who are sometimes attacked by thoughts of such kind as jealousy, envy, revenge, suspicion" and "for the different forms of vexation", which is summed up by Paterson as being used to treat our "prickly" bits.

Balance and Stillness

In contrast to the activity of its energy field, holly exudes a strong feeling of permanence and stillness - it is here and it will remain. This is the reason why it has often been used as a landmark or boundary marker in the past and why, when hedges were trimmed, the hollies were allowed to grow into mature trees, there being some definite connection in the public imagination with being 'holy'.

OAK - The King of the Woods

The Oak has for many of us, even those who think little about trees, a special place. It is probably the first named tree we think of, thus being in the same category as sparrow, Beethoven and apple. Indeed, there are few to whom the acorn and the characteristically-shaped oak leaf are unfamiliar. It has been called 'the king of the woods' and would not be burnt in any ritual fire. The pioneer trees following the last ice age - such as the birch and the hazel - gradually gave way to the oak until much of what is now England was covered with oak forests. Indeed, forests dominated by oak are what most of this country would be covered in if it were not for human intervention - the so-called 'climatic climax'.

Nuttall gives a vivid impression of the form of the tree and of the energy flows underlying it when he writes:

> *"no other tree conveys such an impression of power. In addition to the massiveness of its trunk, its boughs, thick, gnarled and angled, give a special idea of strength in their horizontal branchings. It is also particularly characteristic of them to form 'knees', that is to be zigzag, owing to the fact that lateral instead of terminal buds are apt to carry on the growth. ... The full development of the tree depends on a free access of sunlight; no other tree, indeed, is more insistent on a good light supply."*[89]

Oak

The Most Central and Balanced of Trees

We are all the centre of the universe, but sometimes in our hectic activity we forget it. Oak, perhaps more than any other tree, is still and steady and symbolises presence - an awareness of being the centre of things. It has been called the heart of the woodland, the most complete creative act, and the focus of energy from other trees. People have long sensed this and oaks have been places to congregate for festivity, celebration, religious ceremony and law-making.

Marriage ceremonies have long been held under oaks. As Whitlock says:

> *"Centuries after Christianity became the official religion of England, country couples used to celebrate their marriage under an oak. Eventually the Church forbade it, but even then the couple would go from the church service to dance three times around the oak as ancient custom decreed."* [119]

The district of Gospel Oak in London recalls the existence of an oak which was not only used for preaching the Christian gospel but was also where King Edward the Confessor pledged to keep and defend the laws of England.

The central position of the oak is emphasised by the central month of the year - that in which the Summer Solstice occurs - which was given to the oak under the Celtic calendar.

In some traditions, the Oak King presides over the waxing year, from Yule to Midsummer, and the Holly King over the waning year, from Midsummer to Yule. Battles between the two kings are ritually enacted at the Solstices.

Courage and Strength - The Tree of Endurance and Triumph

Oaks live longer than any other native tree with the exception of the yew, probably over 700 years. This longevity contributes to the wisdom which is ascribed to it. The oak is also strong: surviving for a long time, and it is the tree to which one turns for the strength to carry on. It is not soft, gentle or overly sympathetic, but it will act by en-couraging you to change yourself. It will enfold you in its own strength and in the stillness and certainty which come from realising one's place at the centre of the universe. We need to make the effort, however. When sitting under an oak, I was told that:

> *"We will encourage where we feel this is of benefit to your overall progress - but we will also chastise. We are hard and unmoved. But for those who meet the challenges, we can become joyful and supportive. We can calm and still those who come to us, banishing notions and turning the individual to face the real picture. We present no illusions. We are what we are."*

The Bach remedy for Oak emphasises that it is for those who are brave, "fighting against great difficulties without loss of hope or effort"[8].

A Doorway to Personal Growth

Indeed, taken further, the oak will help us not only to fulfill our true potential but to open the 'doors of perception' to the Otherworld. The Celtic word for oak - 'duir' - is said to have the same roots as the word 'door'. It has been seen as an opening between the two worlds and is symbolised in the triumph of the Oak King, as we have already seen, at Midwinter, and the oak's flowering at Midsummer, both of which stand at the doorway between the two halves of the year, waxing and waning.

Lightning and Mistletoe

The oak is solid and reliable, and yet it is also associated with the unexpected, in the guise of both lightning and mistletoe.

We have already seen how the sky god Zeus was worshipped in the grove of oaks at Dodona in Greece, an area particularly noted for thunderstorms.

This link is emphasised by the frequency with which oak is struck by lightning, as can be seen by the number of "blasted oaks" there are around and their significance in much folklore. The wood of such a tree, for example, was considered powerful and talismans made from it were much sought after. As Lavender and Franklin say :

> "... the oak, tree of ... Zeus, is said to attract lightning. Both Poseidon and Zeus were armed with thunderbolts. ... The oak seems to attract more lightning than any other tree. The Druids would carve a quartered circle on an oak as protection against lightning. In some places in Britain this practice is still maintained by foresters."[59]

Mistletoe is even more unexpected than the lightning strike. Whilst it is associated in the popular mind with oak, because of its link with the Druids, the whole point is that when it was found on oak this was a very rare and special event.

ROWAN - Tree of Sensitivity and Inspiration

Rowan is a hardy tree that grows high up on the mountains, up to 3000 feet in Scotland - higher than any other tree. It can grow in little crevices in the rocks, in the most inhospitable of conditions, and can live for up to 200 years.

Where it is found in woods, these are never pure rowan. It shelters other trees, which then outgrow it and stunt its own

Rowan

further growth, an act of self-sacrifice similar to that of the birch.

However, when rowan has plenty of light and air, it can grow up to 30 feet in height, having slender branches that point upwards. These tend to be fairly permanent and thus allow the rowan's characteristic graceful shape to be maintained.

It has long been known as a very special mystical and magical tree, sometimes called the Wicken tree, a word having the same origin as the word 'witch'.

Rowan has great sensitivity and can sense things in its surroundings, being aware of the subtlest changes in the atmosphere. It is thus good both for psychic protection and for increasing psychic awareness. Emphasising this, rowan berries were used for divining and dowsing and the Welsh used to brew a drink from them which gave 'vision'.

The wood from the rowan was considered to contain all knowledge and wattles (or mats) were woven from it which, when sat on, would give inspiration. There is a phrase - "to go to the wattles of knowledge" - which comes from this.

What rowan seems to do is two-fold - it does increase psychic sensitivity, so that one can know the truth of a situation intuitively. It also inspires - new thoughts and ideas come into the mind, as can the realisation that things previously thought unattainable can actually be achieved.

This sensitivity of the rowan seems to be associated with a particularly large aura, and just by sitting in the aura we can become more sensitive to our surroundings. This can provide protection from psychic attack, as Glennie Kindred advises:

> "If you feel you are under any psychic attack, or being adversely affected by unhelpful influences, gather and wear some Rowan sprays. Hang some over your door.

Spend time with Rowan trees. The Rowan will strengthen your positive life-energy, so that your personal power is so strong you can withstand any negative forces. "[55]

Another name for the rowan is the Quicken tree and this refers to its ability to quicken - to help speed up growth - or alternatively to slow it down if it was too rapid. An example made from rowan was the butter churn, which would quicken the churning of the milk, but would slow the process of turning rancid.

Another aspect of this sensitivity is that rowan seems to flow with its surroundings: it is mutable and will find a way to adapt to whatever inhospitable circumstances it may find itself in. It can withstand hardships, never giving up but holding to the life force within.

It gives strength and hope, encouraging us to take the first step in confidence, allowing that movement of spirit to start which is so necessary if true progress is to be made.

Rowan adds significance to the most ordinary of places, turning it into a point of power, where people will notice it and the sense of place which it creates.

Rowan also has that quality of unexpectedness, turning despair into joy, and we are reminded of the legend where the god Thor was saved from drowning in a rapidly flowing stream by holding on to the branches of a rowan which bent over the water.

SCOTS PINE - The Landmark Tree
Pines are trees of air, from the way in which they appear on hilltops soaring above the other trees to the aromatic resins which permeate the atmosphere around them.

Scots Pine

They grow vertically, shedding their lower branches as they do so, to form a tall straight trunk with the characteristic dark crown of leaves at the top.

Pines can retain moisture in their needles and can thus grow in areas with low rainfall and areas of sandy soil, such as the Breckland area of East Anglia, the nearest thing to a desert which exists in England.

Nuttall refers to the coating of wax over the leaves, which gives a bluish tinge:

> "... *this coloration of the leaves, together with their form, gave the tree a touch of mistiness that tinged it with romance. No doubt it was this mistiness that Tennyson had in mind when he connected the thick, mysterious boughs of the Pine with 'many a cloudy hollow'.*"[89]

With regard to colour, he also says the following:

"A curious and beautiful colour effect may be seen in a ridge of Pines at sunrise. Ruskin pointed out how as the sun rose behind a far distant ridge the sombre leaves and branches of the trees became changed, as by a miracle, into 'one frostwork of intensely brilliant silver', standing out 'like a burning fringe' on either side the sun. Shakespeare before him had noted the sun's transforming touch, -

> 'When from under this terrestrial ball
> He fires the proud tops of the eastern pines.'

and Wordsworth, too, had seen it, -

> *'My thoughts became bright like yon edging of pines*
> *On the steep's lofty verge: how it blackened the air!*
> *But, touched from behind by the sun, it now shines,*
> *With threads that seem part of his own silver hair.'*"[89]

The pine is of air, of the dry places, the high places and the sky. Seen from below, as it usually is, it is seen against the sky and the combination of deep red trunk, dark bluish-green leaves and deep blue sky is very striking, particularly if the pale grey of the daytime moon completes the picture.

The author of "*Cultus Arborum*" says:

> "*The pine was supposed by some to be inhabited by wind spirits, like Ariel, owing to the whispering noises proceeding from it in the breeze.*"[2]

It is therefore to do with ideas, with the spirit and with movement.

Pines are about reaching and attaining, keeping the goal in view, ever encouraging, educating, the direct way of achieving things. It is not emotional or self-analytical. The Bach remedy is given to those who blame themselves and lack confidence. It is adventurous and urges us to put the past behind us and gives us confidence in our abilities. The Scots pine is, above all, uplifting, giving inspiration and excitement. It pulls and inspires new thoughts and new ways of looking at things, uplifting the spirit to new realms. It inspires exciting and creative solutions, bestowing enthusiasm and even joy.

The pine can stand alone. Even in its native forests, the trees are scattered and, in Paterson's words, "creating atmospheric glades with magical depths". It is a tree where solitude is bearable, where silence is sustaining and not threatening.

A place is enlivened by a Scots pine, which adds significance and vitality: our hearts can be similarly moved.

It was the Scots pine that introduced me to the esoteric landscape. The heady mix of ideas about skyways and landmarks which Tony Wedd imparted to me will always mean that the sight of a Scots pine, particularly a solitary and prominent one, gives me a thrill of excitement, which I explain in more detail in Chapter 9.

WILLOW - The Comforter

Of the willow, Nuttall says:

> "To the botanist as well as to the poet the Willow is often a sad subject. There are so many different kinds, their differences are so inconstant, and they will fertilise so much among each other and form hybrid offspring in every intermediate form that the task of distinguishing and grouping them is distracting."[89]

There are many species of willow including almond, bay, crack, goat, grey, purple, weeping and white. Each tends to be very variable and to interbreed readily with the others, making an individual specimen often very difficult to identify.

Willow is attracted by water and is frequently seen in lowland valleys by the side of streams and rivers. It is characterised by branches that rise up to the sky and flexible twigs with leaves that hang down.

The leaves are long and narrow with a pale underside. Because of this, the trees have a rippling appearance when the wind blows through them, and have been likened to the ripples on a body of water.

Sadness

As we have noted, willow has an affinity with water and is thus related to the cycles of the moon, our emotions and feelings. It has long been known as a symbol of grief and deserted or forsaken lovers would wear a garland of willow to mourn for their lost love and to share their sadness with others.

Willow

Comforting

This association with grief is actually because of the comforting properties of willow. It cares for and protects, as a mother, but it is, in essence, a healing tree - healing through strengthening the ability to withstand pain and to refine it. Continuing this theme, it is appropriate that the pain-reliever, aspirin, is derived from willow.

Kindred explains some of the process by which the willow operates:

> *"Sometimes an emotional numbness sets in because the feelings are too painful. The willow teaches us that these feelings must be felt, and brought to the surface. This release is important in order for a person to move through the different levels of sadness, and find inner strength and healing from the experience."*[55]

The Bach remedy also administers to those who find it difficult to accept misfortune without resentment at its unjust nature, and who thus may become bitter and lose interest in life. The Willow remedy would counteract such feelings.[8]

Teaching the Watercourse Way

Willow dissolves away our bitterness and resentment, encourages us to let out our feelings, and to flow with life. In other words, willow teaches the 'Watercourse Way' - one of the names given to Taoism and appropriate to a tree which characteristically lines watercourses.

It is about keeping flexible, like its twigs and leaves, and to flow with life rather than resist it, accommodating rather than confronting. One manifestation of this, which was a way of dealing with sadness, is that willow helped lovers from having jealous thoughts about their lost loves, as well as attracting new love to them.

Enchantment

Willow is also a tree of enchantment. As Paterson says:

> *"The willow-muse is sacred to poets, for the sound of the wind in willow trees exercises a potent influence upon the human mind which results in inspiration. 'Tree-top inspiration' was anciently deemed preferable to intoxication or trance, for it promotes clarity of mind. ... As trees of enchantment, willows formed groves so magical that poets, artists, musicians, priests and priestesses sat within them to gain eloquence, prophecy and inspirational skills through meditation."*[91]

Indeed, *"The Wind in the Willows"*[41] is such a well-known book that we often forget that the title actually means something.

YEW - The Immortal

We saw in Chapter 3 how Allen Meredith, following inspiration directly from the yews, succeeded in demonstrating that they were much older than people had previously thought. Indeed, the yew is now recognised to be not only the oldest of our native trees, but possibly the oldest living thing on Earth, rivalling the Californian bristle-cone pine.

Yews prefer chalky soils, in sheltered locations, occasionally in woods of their own, but more usually in mixed woods. They often grow in the vicinity of beech.

Everlasting Life

Whilst all trees demonstrate this, the yew is pre-eminently the tree of death, transformation, rebirth, immortality and everlasting life. The quotation from Sir George Trevelyan which I reproduce in Chapter 1 shows how the yew can continue indefinitely. This method involves the decay of the

Yew

centre of the original trunk and a new tree growing within, but feeding from the same roots.

Because of this ability to re-grow, the yew is a powerful symbol of regeneration. This is typified by the legend of Naoise and Deidre. They were lovers who died together and were buried side by side. Yew stakes were driven through their corpses by High King Conchobar in order to separate them and to keep their spirits apart. However, the stakes began to sprout and the trees which grew became intertwined above their graves.

In common with other evergreens, the yew also represents life in death, because its leaves are still green at a time when those on other trees have died.

The longevity and everlasting life symbolised by the yew is also present in its wood. It has been said that a post of yew is so resilient that it will outlast a post of iron, and the close grain of the wood, which hardens with age, was the most difficult to work with and that the finest pieces produced by skilled woodworkers were made of yew.

Association with Death

Much of the tradition of immortality has been suppressed with the rise of Christianity and in its place the emphasis on death has predominated. This is due to Christian beliefs about death, which seem to make it something to be feared. The association with churchyards is seen purely in connection with death and legends are told in many places about the way in which the roots of the yew will seek out the mouth of each corpse to gain sustenance. The poisonous nature of much of the tree, including the leaves, bark and seeds, and the use of yew wood for bows and for the hilts of knives have backed up this concentration on death.

Recognition of and Contact with the Past and Future

Because of its longevity and capacity for regeneration, the yew became associated with the past and the ancestors and with the future as well. It is a recognition that the remote past can be with us today and that we can attune to its wisdom by turning within.

The yew was thought to hold the spirits of the ancestors, who could be contacted through the tree. It has thus become particularly associated with the festival of Samhain, when the veil between the worlds is thinnest and the spirits of those who have died can be communicated with most easily.

The Unconscious and the Otherworld: Altered States of Consciousness

In warm weather, the yew gives off a resinous vapour which can give rise to altered states of consciousness, particularly when one is in a whole grove of yews. It is this which the shamans used to inhale to obtain visions. Indeed, at one time, it was thought that if one slept under a yew one would never wake again. Certainly the leaves were one of the ingredients of an incense the smoke of which was used for scrying, but this was always outdoors, as inhaling the smoke was dangerous. We can therefore see that the physical psychoactive properties of the yew itself helped to achieve states of consciousness which enabled individuals to enter the Otherworld.

Yew can also give deeper knowledge and wisdom - the old wisdom that we can find within ourselves. Celtic elders were buried under yews in the belief that their knowledge and wisdom would be transferred to the trees, to be sought in the years ahead. The legendary 'white wand' was cut from yew. It bestowed magical powers and knowledge of the Otherworld, but that knowledge could be dangerous and mean death to those not properly prepared.

Chapter 7

Points of Power

"'You should see them at the full moon', says the deer park keeper, 'the trees look at you in an odd way'."
Thomas Packenham - *Meetings with Remarkable Trees*

Living plants, including trees, were particularly important in ancient times. The yearly cycle of growth, maturity and death was vital to the agricultural community, and the knowledge of when to sow and to harvest was a vital skill, upon which the life of the community depended.

This skill involved knowing when a particular plant had reached one of the 'points of power' in its annual cycle. This concept cannot be clearly defined in physical terms, as it involved seeing with the 'inward eye' and being particularly sensitive as to whether a plant was in a 'growth' or 'decay' phase of its cycle. This was achieved by seeing the aura and the flows of energy within.

Carl Rider, in his excellent book, "*Your Psychic Power*", includes this as one of his exercises. He asks the reader to "give your attention to things and events in nature that are in the process of growing, flourishing, strengthening in some way. And, also, equally, to natural things and events that are decaying, dying, fading or withering".[101]

He then draws attention to the fact that all decaying things, whether it be "a dead bird or a huge old oak", will give you one distinct feeling, and that all growing and blossoming things will produce another feeling.

This sensitivity was clearly highly developed in the ancient people and, indeed, in those of our own day who live close to the earth. And it is something that we can re-learn by paying attention, as Rider has indicated.

We might therefore define the 'points of power' of a plant as being the times of the year when it is at its most powerful and at the peak of its 'growth' phase. For trees, this might be the time when the buds are just forming, the new leaves unfurling, the catkins at their most magnificent, the blossom at its fullest or the autumn leaves and berries at their most colourful. Each tree varies as to which phase or phases are its particular strength or beauty, but these have been generally recognised and marked by people over a long period of time, and the times of year when they occur were noted.

Of course, these dates vary from year to year and place to place, but they generally occurred in the same order and thus marked the passing of the year as a dynamic and direct "calendar" of more immediate use than the fixed framework of the solstices and equinoxes.

There was a natural focus on trees because they were so prominent and permanent and formed the framework which helped determine the whole appearance of the landscape, giving, with successive seasons, a distinctive colour and atmosphere to the whole place.

I doubt whether this was ever an organised system as such, but these 'points of power', when particular trees were most themselves, did mark the turning of the year, and were acknowledged as such by the local people in an area. It was really a recognition of the times of year to focus on particular

trees, incorporating them into the rituals performed at the seasonal festivals.

So, for example, we have already seen the way in which the year was divided into the reigns of the Oak King and the Holly King, and there are many examples, such as the may blossom at Beltane, the elderflowers at Midsummer, and the apples at autumn equinox, where this recognition is an integral part of the seasonal ritual.

This all feels somewhat like a sort of proto-calendar, yet is fundamentally different from the sort of calendar we have today. We base our calendar on the solar year, so that such a date as 12th May, for example, always occurs a set number of days after the spring equinox. This suits our modern purposes well, where meetings are held on the first Monday of the month, or even the first Wednesday after the second Monday! School terms and Committee cycles are fixed at least a year beforehand and summer holidays are often booked several months in advance.

The needs of agriculture are not like this at all. Seasons can be early or late according to the weather and the time for sowing and reaping depends on other factors than calendrical ones in the rigid sense. What is needed is a calendar that responds to the varying seasons. It would vary from place to place and from year to year, and this is not the sort of calendar that can be printed in advance. Therefore, to be effective, the calendrical markers themselves need to vary. They need to be organic - they need to be alive.

This is where the points of power come in. The appearance of the first may blossom, for example, will give a very good idea of where we are in the year and at what stage in the agricultural cycle we have reached. In 1996, I didn't see the first may blossom until 29th May: the following year it was well over a month earlier.

Some writers have gone further than this, and postulated the existence of a Tree Calendar. In recent years, they were brought to public attention through the publication in 1948 of "*The White Goddess*" by Robert Graves, who describes his discovery of a tree calendar in the following terms:

"I first found the Beth-Luis-Nion tree-alphabet in Roderick O'Flaherty's Ogygia; he presents it ... as a genuine relic of Druidism orally transmitted down the centuries. It is said to have been latterly used for divination only and consists of five vowels and thirteen consonants. Each letter is named after the tree or shrub of which it is the initial:

Beth	B	*Birch*
Luis	L	*Rowan*
Nion	N	*Ash*
Fearn	F	*Alder*
Saille	S	*Willow*
Uath	H	*Hawthorn*
Duir	D	*Oak*
Tinne	T	*Holly*
Coll	C	*Hazel*
Muin	M	*Vine*
Gort	G	*Ivy*
Pethboc	P	*Dwarf Elder*
Ruis	R	*Elder*
Ailm	A	*Silver Fir*
Onn	O	*Furze*
Ur	U	*Heather*
Eadha	E	*White Poplar*
Idho	I	*Yew*

The names of the letters in the modern Irish alphabet are also those of trees, and most of them correspond with O'Flaherty's list, though T has become gorse; O, broom; and A, elm.

I noticed almost at once that the consonants of this alphabet form a calendar of seasonal tree-magic, and that all the trees figure prominently in European folklore."[42]

Doreen Valiente recounts how "*The White Goddess*" was written:

"The way in which Robert Graves came to write this book, according to him, was unusual. It took the form of 'a sudden overwhelming obsession' which compelled him to suspend work on the historical novel he had set out to write, in favour of discovering the inner meaning of a mysterious old Welsh poem called The Battle of the Trees. In three weeks, he tells us, he had written a 70,000-word book, called at first The Roebuck in the Thicket but which eventually became The White Goddess. His mind worked so furiously, he says, under the influence of this inspiration, that his pen could scarcely keep pace with it."[112]

Ogham was an inscribed symbolic language, probably pre-Celtic in origin, consisting of strokes carved into stone or staves of wood. Philip Carr-Gomm refers to it as "a particular method for comm-unicating and remembering their wealth of tree-knowledge". Each stroke can be considered a letter of the 'alphabet' and represented the first letter of the tree which was ascribed to it. He says:

"Although we know the letters that each stroke represents, and can translate the ancient Ogham inscriptions accordingly, we cannot be so confident when we come to associate the trees with particular months.

There has been much controversy as to whether the Ogham really was used as a calendar by the Druids, linking each tree and letter of the alphabet to a moon month, as suggested by Robert Graves. Whilst it is important to be aware that there is controversy, it is also important to understand that Druidry is evolving, and that if they didn't correlate them in 500BC they do now - if it was Robert Graves' invention, then he was acting as a Druid when he did so - he was inspired in other words. Someone has to invent things, or 'receive' them from the invisible world, and just because he or she does so in AD 1948 rather than BC 1948 is in the final analysis unimportant to those of us who want to use Druidry as a living system, as opposed to those who want to study its origins for a purely academic purpose."[20]

I have no intention of examining Ogham in depth because, although it was integral to the relationship between the Celts, and possibly pre-Celts, and the trees they were living with, it need not be so for us and it may divert us into by-ways that are no doubt fascinating but which take us away from our central theme - our own experience of the trees themselves.

It is probably best to look at the various versions of the tree calendar as being myths pointing towards the underlying truth of the trees' points of power throughout the year. As Philip Carr-Gomm says:

"... since we have no physical proof of how or whether the early Druids made these connections, it seems important to allow our own inner sensibilities to guide us, and to be aware of the fact that writers disagree. The important thing is that we should establish our own personal relationship with the trees and their spirits. If we fill ourselves with other people's ideas about which trees are sacred and what properties they possess or symbolise, it tends to block our own intuitive impressions."[20]

The essence of what Philip Carr-Gomm is saying - that we should establish our own personal relationship with the trees and their spirits - is, as far as I am concerned, the key to the whole thing and what I have been trying to emphasise in this book.

So, it may be more fruitful to set the arguments aside and to go out each month, perhaps at Full Moon, and see which trees are in flower, fruit or otherwise prominent, and make our own calendar, realising that it will only be accurate in terms of actual dates in the year that we make it. But the whole point is that you will be noticing the inter-relationships between the different 'points of power' which can then be used to guide your ritual year - an effective supplement to a printed calendar.

It is important to stress that this doesn't have to be complete: it is something you can work on over several years - something that will be meaningful to your own locality, so that you will learn, for example, which hawthorn tree comes out into flower first and watch for that as a marker of the seasons. At the very least it will add significance to your walks in the area around where you live.

If you want more of a fixed calendar, the most practicable thing is to follow the cycles of the moon. You will find that, even with the annual variation in the seasons, each month (by which I mean the period from one new moon to the next) will have a particular quality to it, which you might want to name - a name which sums up what is happening to the landscape around you. Anything more detailed is probably too rigid to reflect the realities of our environment.

Chapter 8

In the Depths of the Wild Wood

"There was certainly something erotic in them, as there is in all places that isolate and hide; but woods are in any case highly sensuous things."

John Fowles - *The Tree*

The Experience of Woods

Woods are special to most of us, as if we know from deep within ourselves that deep within them are answers to questions that we have scarcely begun to formulate. Certainly, woods have had a profound effect on most of us and been the source of much inspiration. Indeed, many of us had our first experience of the numinous - that living spirit which lies behind physical form - through walking in the woods. This is so universal in those I have talked to that I suspect it to be of a fundamental and archetypal nature, and there is certainly an almost archetypal quality about many descriptions of how individuals were attracted to the woods at a very young age and how some of their deepest experiences occurred there.

Kiri Clay-Egerton gives an account entitled *'Idylls and Griefs of the Wild Wood'* which illustrates this well:

"When I was a child my parents read the story of "The Wind in the Willows" to me, and I suppose this is where the attraction for the Wild Wood started. ... I loved nothing more than to walk in small quiet woods drinking in deeply of the power of towering trees, which to me resembled processional archways to a majestic roof way above my head. In spring this roof whispered and shook gently as it unfolded itself into being, after the bare branches of winter. Before the roof canopy was complete in summer, I used to play in Nature's Cathedral, in and out of the tree trunks, sometimes in the deep chiaroscuro of shade and at other times dancing in and out of the slanting beams of sunlight like an overweight human sprite. ... I have never known the words to justify descriptions of the colours I encountered - brown, green and grey are in no way evocative of what I knew and loved. The colours and textures of the individual strands of the woodland tapestry of trees only teased and tempted me on to explore the tiny glades of colour. My feet stopped at the very edge of a scented, gently swaying carpet of blue bells; who was I, a mortal child, to defile this sacred place? Suddenly my admiration of such beauty vanished as I toppled over, either tripped up by a tree root or pushed by a laughing sprite. There on this blue carpet all I could do was to gaze upward into the greenery above, and observe in my turn those who had till then gained amusement from my stumbling progress through their domain."[26]

Richard St. Barbe Baker, who in his long lifetime did more than most people to increase public awareness of trees, their life and their function, gives the following account of his experience of the wild wood in his youth:

"At first there was a path to which I kept as it wound its way down into the valley, but presently I found myself in the thick wood where the trees were taller and the path was lost in bracken beneath the pines. Soon I was

completely isolated in the luxuriant, tangled growth of bracken which was well over my head. In my infant mind it seemed the fairyland of my dreams. I wandered on, as one does in a dream - and lost all sense of time and space. Every now and then, when I looked up, I could see the sunshine coming through the tops of the tall pines, casting subtle shadows on the continuous canopy of the fern fronds, which were bright green over me. Their pungent scent was a delight to me. Although I could only see a few yards ahead, I had no sense of being shut in. The sensation was exhilarating and I began to walk faster, buoyed up with an almost ethereal feeling of well-being, as if I had been detached from the earth. I became intoxicated by the beauty around me and was immersed in joyousness and exultation, to feel I was a part of it all."[9]

The Society of Trees

This chapter is about what might be called the "community" or "society" of trees and what happens when they stand and grow together. Trees cannot be seen in isolation from the land in which they are growing, or from other trees, for they, like us, are social beings. We have a need for both society and solitude. This need varies in each of us and it is important for our health that our desires to be alone and to be with other people are satisfied for us as individuals. Trees are the same in this respect - and yet, they cannot move as we can and get away from others if they feel the need to be on their own.

I think the answer to this lies in the relationship between the species and the individual tree. Trees of the same species can interact with each other provided that they are within a certain distance of each other. This communication seems to operate, at least partly, through the medium of the wind. It is certainly possible to recognise the sounds made as the wind passes through different types of tree. Thomas Hardy clearly

understood this, as revealed in the opening paragraph of
"Under the Greenwood Tree":

> *"To dwellers in a wood almost every species of tree has its
> voice as well as its feature. At the passing of the breeze
> the fir-trees sob and moan no less distinctly than they
> rock; the holly whistles as it battles with itself; the ash
> hisses amid its quiverings; the beech rustles while its flat
> boughs rise and fall. And winter, which modifies the note
> of such trees as shed their leaves, does not destroy its
> individuality."*[45]

It seems likely, then, that trees can be sensitive, via their
subtle bodies, to this wind movement and sound generation
from another tree and can, at some level, recognise others of
their type. A friend has told me she received, when tuning in
to a particular beech tree that the tree is never alone if it is
within wind-whistling distance of another beech. Indeed, one
of the principles that I accepted when writing Chapter 6 was
that one could tune in to all beeches, for example, by tuning in
to one particular example wherever one happened to be.

Similarly, I feel that the needs of solitude and community can
be met for the species as a whole if individuals of that species
are in isolated spots or growing close together. And, of course,
the needs of different species will vary in this respect. It is
rather like my habitual answer to some such question as:
"Wouldn't you like to go on a visit to Australia?", which is:
"Well, somebody else has done it, so I don't need to!".

We shall be looking at solitary trees in the next chapter. In
this one, we are looking at trees in society - in other words,
woods and forests. Whatever we have said about trees is even
more true for woods, because woods are the society of trees,
and to the extent that the quality of a society is more than the
sum of the individuals making it up, so the character of a
wood is far more than that of the individual trees that can be
found there. Woods are not just a collection of trees in close

proximity - they are something far more. They are entities in their own right. The individual trees that make them up have their own spirit and aura which interacts with other trees in its vicinity to create something which has a different quality from the individual tree, just as a community has a character distinct from the individuals who make it up.

There is something very special about a wood - particularly an ancient wood: it has a life of its own. Indeed, some can still be found which have never known the plough, being remnants of the primaeval forest. On entering such a wood we come into the very presence of the God and the Goddess. Even if we cannot see them, woods are a haven for the nature spirits, and part of us can certainly sense and interact with them.

Alíen Land and Sanctuary - A Place Between the Worlds

The wood has been a common literary subject, as John Fowles has emphasised:

> "It is not for nothing that the ancestors of the modern novel that began to appear in the early Middle Ages so frequently had the forest for setting and the quest for central theme ... the metaphorical forest is constant suspense, stage awaiting actors: heroes, maidens, dragons, mysterious castles at every step."[36]

The wood always seems to have two sides to it - an alien land, which we can never really be part of; and a sanctuary which will welcome us, where we can talk with the nature spirits and the dryads. They are somewhere to escape to, where one can hide and, in Lorenz' phrase, can "see without being seen". Everything you needed was in the wood and, characteristically, Robin Hood - the noble outlaw - chose a forest in which to live. Indeed, John Fowles has expressed it this way:

"All through history trees have provided sanctuary and refuge for both the justly and the unjustly persecuted and hunted. In the wood I know best there is a dell, among beeches, at the foot of a chalk cliff. Not a person a month goes there now, since it is well away from any path. But three centuries ago it was crowded every Sunday, for it is where the Independants came, from miles around along the border of Devon and Dorset, to hold their forbidden services. There are freedoms in woods that our ancestors perhaps realized more fully than we do. I used this wood, and even this one particular dell, in The French Lieutenant's Woman, for scenes that it seemed to me, in a story of self-liberation, could have no other setting."[36]

As representative of the two approaches - alien land and welcoming sanctuary - I want to examine just two modern novels - *"Mythago Wood"* by Robert Holdstock[52] and *"The Herb of Grace"* by Elizabeth Goudge[40].

Mythago Wood

"Mythago Wood" is a strange story about Ryhope Wood - a wood which protects itself. One cannot go far in before becoming disoriented and finding oneself back at the edge again very quickly. In the book, the hero's father, George Huxley, following a meeting with the discoverer of leys, Alfred Watkins, had measured an energy in the oakwoods:

"... an energy associated with all the life that grew there. He had found a spiral vortex around each tree, a sort of aura, and those spirals bounded not just trees, but whole stands of trees, and glades."[52]

His brother, Christian, explained further:

"The old man believed that all life is surrounded by an energetic aura - you can see the human aura as a faint

glow in certain light. In these ancient woodlands, primary woodlands, the combined aura forms something far more powerful, a sort of creative field that can interact with our unconscious. And it's in the unconscious that we carry what he calls the pre-mythago - that's myth imago, the image of the idealized form of a myth creature. The image takes on substance in a natural environment, solid flesh, blood, clothing, and - as you saw - weaponry. The form of the idealized myth, the hero figure, alters with cultural changes, assuming the identity and technology of the time. When one culture invades another - according to father's theory - the heroes are made manifest, and not just in one location! Historians and legend-seekers argue about where Arthur of the Britons, and Robin Hood really lived and fought, and don't realize that they lived in many sites. And another important fact to remember is that when the mind image of the mythago forms it forms in the whole population ...and when it is no longer needed, it remains in our collective unconscious, and is transmitted through the generations."[52]

Both intimate physical contact and warfare takes place between the humans and the mythagos which, in my opinion, takes it beyond what could actually happen, but then it is a work of fiction (or Fiction/Fantasy, as it is described on the cover). Certainly the talk of energies, auras, vortexes and interaction is very much how many sensitives have seen the Wild Wood.

The Herb of Grace

"The Herb of Grace" is a very different book, a moving tale of human emotion set in the landscape around the old house of Damerosehay, near the Hampshire coast. The great Knyghtwood is not just a backdrop for the story, but a part of it. Despite misgivings, many of the characters in the book

found, perhaps by accident, places in the wood that were special to them, some only going in a little way and others much further. The young twins, Jerry and José, are the ones who had been furthest in:

""With Jill we've been as far as the big oak," said Jerry. "And with Ben we've been as far as his special place, where the Person is who plays the pipes; but with you we're going right deep in to the Place Beyond, where the Fairy Person with the horns is." ... "Who is this Fairy Person?" she asked.

"We saw his pointy face looking at us out of the wood that first day we came," said José. "We couldn't see more of him because he was hiding in a holly-tree. Then he went away, and we haven't seen him again. We want to."

"What's the Place Beyond?" asked Sally.

"What the other places aren't," said Jerry, a little impatient with her stupidity.

"But how will you know it when you get there?" persisted the obtuse Sally. "I mean, there are so many places that aren't what other places are."

The twins looked at her pityingly.

"Because it isn't many places, it's one place. It's in the middle.... "They very soon passed the oak-tree that was Nadine's place; it wasn't very deep in. And they crossed over the first little bridge to Ben's Brockis Island, and the second little bridge to the deeper bit of the wood beyond. And they came to the stream that was Sally's place, with the break in the bog-myrtle bushes to the left that led to Annie-Laurie's place; and then they were in a part of the wood where none of the others had ever yet been. Even Jill, though she had run about Knyghtwood often as a *little girl, had not been as far as this for many years, and she looked about her with the interest of a traveller in a strange country."*[40]

Deeper in the wood, its character changes:

"It became deeper and more mysterious. There were no more birches, wild crab-apples and hawthorns. The oak-trees still persisted, but they were much larger, and among them were those splendid knights of the forest, the armoured beeches. The hollies, old as the conquest, grew to a great height here, they had more berries on them and their polished leaves sparkled with reflected light."[40]

They went along a narrow path between steeply rising banks where great beeches and ferns grew until they came to a "great rampart of holly" which blocked their way. Seeing a rabbit go that way they remembered that there was a small tunnel through the holly which was "extremely prickly, damp, dark and uncomfortable" but which they could crawl through.

""How does the Person with the Horns get in?" she wondered aloud, as they paused to get their breath and remove prickles out of themselves. "He couldn't get through here."

"Jumps over the top," said Jerry. "He's a Fairy Person. He can jump as high as the moon.""[40]

They came through to a sheltered hollow, surrounded by a thicket of holly and yew which had grown up in the previous hundred years. There was a green lawn with a stream running through it, with the ruins of a chapel adjacent. The animals and birds were unafraid, as the place felt like a sanctuary.

"The sunset deepened all about them. The sky above, feathered and delicately tinted with small clouds of

saffron and rose-pink, bent over them like the arched wings of a bird, and in the stream below, in every polished leaf and blade of grass, the glory was reflected. ... The berries on the holly-bushes that stood one on each side of the ruined chapel glowed like a thousand lamps, and within the light shone more and more brightly, and made a gold path from the door to the children's feet.

Hand in hand they trod the bright path through the warm and golden air, and came to the ruined chapel, and hand in hand they went inside."[40]

When they found Jill again, Jerry was carrying a great branch of holly:

" ... whose berries were so bright and lovely that even those in Jill's basket looked a little dim in comparison, and José clutched (wonderful for December) a tiny bunch of wild white violets.

"They were growing inside," she said.

Jill did not ask inside where - she did not, like Sally, question them as to where they had been or what they had seen. She knew how worrying, even how agonizing sometimes, the questions of grown-ups can be to children, whose capacity for experience so far outstrips their capacity for talking about it ..."[40]

This account, which is well worth reading in full, is very moving and is the sort of thing which many of us, though perhaps to a lesser extent, have experienced for ourselves.

Dwelling Places of the Spirit

"*Mythago Wood*" and "*The Herb of Grace*" both present qualities of the wood which are based on real experiences -

above all, perhaps, that woods and forests are the dwelling-places of the spirit, the natural home of those inhabitants of the Otherworld with whom we share the Earth.

As an example of this, not too far from where I live is an area of ancient woodland - generally recognised to be a survival of primaeval forest that has never seen the plough. Immediately on entering the wood, even during the daytime, there is a tremendous power which can be sensed by many. It has a very definite boundary but, once within, one is freed from the present-day and can wander in both space and time.

Large spreading oaks in open grassland are the most striking feature - one half expects Robin Hood to come riding by! But adjoining this is a thicker, denser wood with large old holly trees, great beeches, hawthorns, ash, birch and many more besides.

Kati-Ma Koppana, the Finnish pagan writer, recounts a similar feeling, characterising her experience of the spirit of the forests in terms of the Goddess:

> *"The birch trees gleam whitely, white as bone, among the darker fir and spruce. It is autumn and the leaves are yellow, drifting softly down like golden sequins from an old Indian wedding veil.*
>
> *You feel that someone is watching you as you approach the edge of the birch grove - but there is no one there. Wandering in to the forest you lose your way, and all the time there are eyes watching you, eyes all around, yet you cannot see them. You sit down and the feeling is in your head. What is this strange sensation, this power, welling up in you and around you?*
>
> *The forest spirit, the soul of the forest. That quality which the Ancient Greeks tried to tie down in hamadryads, in the goddess Artemis. And in this country*

of Finland we also have such a goddess - we call her Mielikki."[57]

It seems clear from the above and from many other accounts of people's experiences that the wood, and particularly the wild primaeval wood, is in reality a gateway to the Otherworld, or, to use a phrase which has often been used to describe the magic circle - a place "between the worlds".

Indeed, in writing this chapter, I want to acknowledge my indebtedness to Robin Ellis, who has permitted me to quote at length from an article of his entitled *"The Woods between the Worlds"*[35]. It is expressed in a clear and moving way and accords totally with my thoughts and feelings on these matters. He refers to "certain woods and forests" where something infinitely stranger is at work than in "normal" woodland, which he describes as "a sort of creative Otherworld power that seems to be able to interact with the human unconscious". I suspect strongly that most of these are the old primaeval forests which over long ages of time have built up a powerful spirit presence which most of us, whether consciously or not, are able to "tune into" in certain circumstances. He says : "Such woodlands are comparatively rare, but they represent a tremendous source of spiritual power to us, if we can cope with them! They are not the easiest of places to be in."

Robin Ellis continues:

> *"Once within the deep woods however, you will notice a distinct change in the atmosphere. In this part of the forest you seem to stand in an old, strange, and solemn universe all of its own. Before you can 'go between the worlds', however, your consciousness has to align itself with that of the Wildwood! What happens is that the wood begins to haunt you. Trees seem to move by themselves; the wood becomes preternaturally dark; strange, disturbing sounds are heard from various*

*directions; at night there are strange lights seen glowing
in the darkness. If you can put up with all this, you
might possibly be able to 'cross over' from the deep woods
of our world, into the Wildwood itself!*

*This should be seen as an Otherworld journey - and it is
a little uncertain as to how much of it is literally
happening, and how much is subjective experience.
However, there is a QUALITY about the Wildwood that
defies experience! The size of certain trees is unbelievable,
bigger than anything seen in our time. The woodland is
totally natural, with no sign of it having been trimmed or
coppiced. The giant trees are invariably oak, and enfold
whole areas of underwood. The leaf cover is so complete
that it blocks out the sky. The undergrowth is thin, and
walking is easy, but it is dimly lit. The whole wood
radiates an overwhelming Otherworld power! There is a
great abundance of oak and hazel, but with whole
strands of ash and beech, and other trees which do not
normally grow together. So the Wildwood is not 'natural'
at all. It is a hundred forests in one."[35]*

Kiri Clay-Egerton is also aware of this change of atmosphere.
She says:

*"I was always glad to go deeper into the apparent gloom
because I would be beyond one of the woodland's outer
barriers; once I was beyond it then I forgot those who
quite possibly waited for me to emerge."*

In another piece, she gives an account of what she calls "A
Cathedral Forest", which certainly has characteristics similar
to those reported by Robin Ellis:

*"One day I went for a walk that certainly was not a
normal one. I found myself in a totally different kind of
wooded area. Here my feet trod upon a pathway with a
spongy texture. It was a joy to walk upon: I felt that here*

I could walk all day long and not suffer from sore and/or tired feet. On either side my path was bordered as far as I could see, both behind and in front of me, by soaring tree trunks. These trunks appeared to rise straight and tall for may tens of feet into the heavens above. They were not marred by any sign of lower branches or twigs but resembled soaring, living colonnades holding up a vast and barely discerned ceiling.

As I walked upon this spongy path or aisleway, I became aware that these trees appeared to me to be ageless. I could not really discern young trees from old or mature ones, or from each other. They did not actually look like anything I knew, or had encountered before, even in pictures. They were still alive (I could feel their slow breathing) but even for trees they had slowed down their life-cycles so much that life for them was merely ticking over. Their life was extremely slow but precise and their age had robbed them of nothing, and in fact only added to the sense of majesty which surrounded them. I understood that it was not actually time that had aged them but the veneration of countless generation who trod these pathways between these living columns of tree trunks.

To me this was a place that had obviously been held as a sacred area for so very long now that it had in its turn breathed this very atmosphere itself and so projected this onto a mind which was prepared or conditioned to be both sympathetic and empathetic to various woodlands and their forms of existence. ... it resembled what I might envisage as a naturally constructed 'Cathedral'. Here lived and breathed holiness and beauty ..."[26]

I have written elsewhere about Dingley Dell, but it follows on so well from the above descriptions that I have no hesitation in mentioning it again here. It is located on the edge of a large northern city, in that intermediate zone where the miles of solid built-up housing give way to fields, on a rise that enables one to look out over the whole city. The area once consisted of large detached houses in their own grounds. One of the grandest was demolished a few years ago - perhaps in expectation of the planning permission for housing development that has not so far been forthcoming.

The grounds were large and had been extensively planted with trees at least 200 years ago. They have been neglected for many years. There had also been an orchard and an extensive belt of planting along the north side of the site.

A friend was led there by "chance" a few years ago and was amazed by the feel of the place. She started to go there to meditate and still uses it regularly. I was taken there for the first time at dusk and followed the path round as the sun was setting and the sky gradually turned dark. This seems to be the right time of day to go there as the "normal" magical atmosphere is greatly intensified.

One enters the land through a small gap next to the footpath and immediately there is a feeling of wildness - suburbia is left far behind. Ahead is a tall beech tree. One instinctively senses that this is the guardian of the site and it is natural to stop here for a few minutes before going on. The tree likes to be embraced and it takes three of us, holding hands, to make a ring around its trunk. There are holly trees here as well, with girths thicker than I have ever seen. Holly grows very slowly and I have begun to suspect that this may date back much further than we had ever thought.

Moving on, one goes through an avenue of yews. It is natural to walk slowly, taking up a natural rhythmic gait, as if in walking meditation. Entering the yew avenue is to enter into the dark - that passageway through to the Otherworld. Everyone instinctively falls silent. To one side is a large old yew tree, its branches low down on the ground. One realises that here is somewhere very special and protected. It is possible to feel the aura surrounding this tree/place physically and there is a definite barrier which will admit or not as it wills. Within the confines of the tree one feels protected, with a heightened sensitivity to one's surroundings. One begins to be aware of the interest of nature spirits.

Reluctantly moving on, we reach the far side of the wood, close to a modern motor road. The traffic noise does not intrude, however, as we turn to start the walk back. Here is one of the wonders of this place - a great belt of mature trees. Hornbeams, taller and straighter than I have ever seen before, together with beech and oak.

The path winds its way between these huge trunks, coming up to meet each one in turn, and then changing direction as it passes - a succession of small clearings and thickets alternate. The light of the setting sun reflects off the bark of these large beings - one can sense the Earth Spirit in this place, and one falls silent in awe and joy. The regular rhythm of the path and the trees induces a state of mind quite different from the everyday and it is in a totally different frame of mind that one finds oneself back at the sentinel beech.

It is a very special place and I am privileged to have been taken there.

Robin Ellis writes movingly about what he describes as an eerie part of Sherwood - the Forest of Bilhaugh:

"Grey, gnarled and knotty oaks form a kind of processional way into this forest, from the old, sacred, 'Fanny Grove' (now a picnic site). This old realm of trees (the forest of Bilhaugh with Meanby Birkland) extends for two or three miles, and it is dominated by old oaks, with huge, barkless trunks, and twisted branches. Some of these oak trees are as much as eighty feet high, bare and black, scarred by lightning and storms, and many of them split from top to bottom - and yet their branches are

full of foliage. The surface of the ground is covered in ferns, mosses, bluebells, violets and foxgloves in their season. In the summer the gorse, smelling of delicious odours, flourishes under the wide foliage of the trees. Grass snakes sun themselves in the glades, and the whole forest resounds with the melody of birds. As always a strange atmosphere can be felt. A feeling that this place is outside normal time, in a universe of its own! On a summer's night, when the shadows cast by the moon enhance the ghostly magic of the place, it is filled with the mystery of the Otherworld! Hares, rabbits and hedgehogs are seen in abundance - and the cry of the night-owl can be heard from the far off dells of Birkland, echoing from glade to glade throughout the night.

This is a magical place. It is said that 'Bilhaugh is worth travelling a hundred miles barefoot to see, and once seen, it can never be forgotten!' And many have come to see, and to spend many days in this haunted wilderness, which seems to be of great extent! Pemberton the Wanderer walked all the way from London to spend one day here, and then returned, praising God that he was still strong enough to make 'so beautiful a pilgrimage!'

None of the many that came believed this to be an ordinary place, or to be like the other forests that they knew. One man said that he had been many a year in the backwoods of the American continent, and seen many a famous forest in England, but he had never known what a tree was until he had seen the giants of Bilhaugh!

In this ancient forest - with its visitors centre and tourists swarming around the Major Oak - queer things have happened, and continue to happen, to people from time to time."[35]

Concealment and Confusion

Perhaps the most obvious quality of a wood is that, as you enter it, you feel that you are going inside, and we feel a bit the same way that we do when we go inside a building, in that there is a roof and walls. Admittedly, this effect is more pronounced in the summer, with the leafy canopy as the roof and the walls represented by our inability to see very far.

It is much easier to hide (and indeed to get lost) in a wood than outside and we see again its attraction for outlaws. Lorenz' observation, which I quote in Chapter 4, about the advantages of being able to see without being seen, referred specifically to the edge of a wood. Because of the differing light conditions, it is easy to see out but very difficult for anyone outside to see in.

This leads on to the wood being a place of secrets and concealment. John Fowles makes the point that "there are freedoms in the woods". They are places for lovers' trysts and May eve revelries, and indeed, many pagan rituals still take place in woods, where they are free from prying eyes. The trees themselves cut us off from the outside world: they make us look at close quarters, both at the wood itself and at ourselves.

The light is also different because it is filtered through the leaves and branches and, just like the light from the Full Moon, everything it shines upon changes to a more magical state.

A feature of woods which springs naturally from their enclosed inward-looking quality and opportunities for concealment is that of disorientation in time and space. We lose our sense of direction, and our awareness of time, far more easily in a wood, and it is frequently expressed in terms of some conscious quality of the wood itself, as C.S. Lewis points out:

"... if you know anything about woods, you will know that one is always finding imaginary paths. They disappear after about five minutes and then you think you have found another (and hope it is not another but more of the same one) and it also disappears, and after you have been well lured out of your right direction you realize that none of them were paths at all."[62]

Robin Ellis confirms this:

"You may find yourself walking in a totally different direction to that which you had intended. At times it is almost possible to experience the switch in direction. The deep woods are well defended! If you try to force your way through, you find yourself walking in elaborate circles, even though you are convinced that you are walking in a straight line!"[35]

I have also noted, over a period of time, certain changes to a wood which cannot easily be explained in the usual way. It is as if our mind is being shown certain things and denied others, so that, for example, you may think it is going to be ever so easy to find a particular tree again, perhaps one that you have chosen for a special purpose. But then, when you go back some time later, things are subtly different: the trees seem to have moved and you can be left confused and uncertain unless you accept this as part of the nature of the woods, their own way of protecting their secrets.

Disorientation in time can also occur, as Allen Meredith found when visiting a grove of ancient yews in Surrey:

"Allen has twice found that he has 'stepped out of time' while in Druid's Grove - that when he has left the grove his watch has shown the same time as when he entered it, despite the watch apparently working perfectly."[24]

Attunement and Changes of Consciousness

We can learn from woods as we can learn from trees. In many ways, the lessons are magnified and are easier to take in, because of the number and variety of trees present. But, as with the individual tree, it helps if we genuinely ask permission to enter first. Kiri Clay-Egerton describes what often happens:

> "It seemed to be held in place by what appeared, at least to me, as a thick impenetrable undergrowth boundary. If one was, however, given leave or licence to enter the area then this insurmountable barrier parted to allow you through, much in the same way as a knife cuts through butter."[26]

Attunement and giving yourself up to the wood also helps, as Kati-Ma Koppana makes clear:

> "Anybody at all can go for a walk in the forest, walk quietly and enjoy its beauty, but at a certain point in our journey we must go deeper into the heart of the forest, not merely to see its tall trees, its undergrowth and the path winding forward between it all, but the inner place ... In approaching a forest one must change one's attitude. Forget about being safe in the forest as it can be dangerous. It can trip you up, lose you along the winding paths which might simply wind out again ... The forest may confuse you by putting the same large rock in three different places. Forget safety and replace it with TRUST. If you trust the forest, it will trust you."[58]

In other words, with right attunement, the disorientation that C.S. Lewis, Robin Ellis and others have encountered need not be an issue. Our minds, our consciousness, can be changed when we are in the wood, because it is apart from the world, like another state of being, just as the dream state is.

Robin Ellis advocates spending time in these haunted forests, with long periods of meditation. saying "...it is a journey as much into your own soul as it is into the silent reaches of the forest, and none have made the Otherworld journey into the Wildwood and have returned unchanged by the experience."[35]

Just as entering a wood cuts us off from the outside world and its concerns, so, when we leave a wood, there is a very definite feeling of returning to everyday reality. It is like having visited another country.

We know that we come into the presence of great wisdom when we enter a wood, though we may not be able to articulate what we have learned.

Woods as a Learning Experience

Traditionally, learning took place in the landscape - not just about the landscape itself, but using the landscape as a medium for other teaching, as David Clarke and Andy Roberts' contact in the Yorkshire Dales made clear:

> *"At the time of my 'awakening', as we called it, my maternal grandmother was responsible for passing on the teachings ... and this at first took the form of what might be called 'nature walks' ... in which we would walk for miles in all weathers, at all times of year and at all times of day and night. ... slowly I began to realize just what I was being taught. Slowly from being a series of roads, paths, fields and hills, I began to see the general topography of the area in which I lived in a very different way altogether. There were no physical barriers to us and we would roam freely, paying little attention to the recognized rights of way or easy ways across the countryside, but instead paying total attention to the land and how it was formed, its shapes, textures and hidden places. Instead of land to be swiftly passed*

through on the way to somewhere else, it was revealed to me as part of the body of a living thing whose mysteries were accessible if you looked in the right way, at the right time. And as we walked, she would point out and name certain landscape features which were important to the learning, and I came to know them by those names."[25]

Of course, there was much to learn in the wood - the medicinal and psychoactive properties of various plants, trees and fungi being an obvious example. And yet, the wood was also used as a medium for teaching and learning in another sense, and this has a lot to do with the way in which we learn. The words 'beech' and 'book' have the same roots. At one level, this has been explained in terms of the suitability of beech as a material for writing on, but it also points us in the direction of a deeper truth - that of the wood or forest itself as a medium for teaching and learning.

What we learn seems to be enhanced by its association with something outside itself, including where we were when we were being taught. The eye alights on some feature of our environment, and then, later, when that particular feature is glimpsed, it reminds us of what we were learning at the time.

In fact, it is often done in a very organised way, with a route through the forest, with stopping points, reminiscent of the Stations of the Cross in Christian tradition, where specific teachings are imparted. Originally there may have been an elaborate network of paths through the woods linking special trees which formed something like a physical representation of the Qabalah, whereby the points and the paths were both of significance.

Progress would have been slow - a form of walking meditation - and the walk would have been arranged so that certain things were seen and then concealed. These would have perhaps included unusual-shaped branches, intertwined trees, simulacra in the bark and other more unusual things - all with the implicit intention of implanting on the memory an image of the place where something was learned.

This, I must emphasise, may not have been formal teaching. If, as I am suggesting, the wood is an entity in its own right, in some cases an ancient and wise being, then merely to place oneself in its presence enables the spirit to absorb some of that wisdom. All that the human teacher can do is to lead the pupil by the hand, perhaps pointing out certain features of the wood which have specific significance only if one were in an appropriately altered state of consciousness.

I am not referring to anything which would seem the slightest bit unusual to the native peoples of many parts of the world. If we think it is an odd way of learning, that is merely because we in urbanised, civilised society have largely lost that instinctive response to the land - but we can re-learn it.

My own experience was of being taken through a wood and being told of things that had happened at different spots along the path. These were not in any way special to the outward eye, but they had significance and it was this significance which was passed on - it helped to bring the wood alive or rather make me more aware of its living quality.

A gateway to the Otherworld and a true centre of learning - these are some of the ways in which we interact with woods. Of course, they are a lot more than that: they have their own society, their own being and their own activity which is far removed from the human realm. But to the extent that we can be affected by the wood as we open ourselves up, it is still the place to be in order to most fully experience the wild quality of tree spirit.

Chapter 9

Enchanted Places

"They walked on, thinking of This and That, and by-and-by they came to an enchanted place on the very top of the Forest called Galleons Lap, which is sixty-something trees in a circle; and Christopher Robin knew that it was enchanted because nobody had ever been able to count whether it was sixty-three or sixty-four, not even when he tied a piece of string round each tree after he had counted it. Being enchanted, its floor was not like the floor of the Forest, gorse and bracken and heather, but close-set grass, quiet and smooth and green. It was the only place in the Forest where you could sit down carelessly, without getting up again almost at once and looking for somewhere else. Sitting there they could see the whole world spread out until it reached the sky, and whatever there was all the world over was with them in Galleon's Lap."

A.A. Milne - *The House at Pooh Corner*

We have seen how trees have points of power, times of the year when they are at their strongest and when they most fully express their own inner nature. Yet time is only one of the factors: equally as potent is location. Trees have individual personalities - and one significant influence on this is where they are.

Trees do not just grow naturally: indeed, most of those in existence today (certainly in this country) have been planted.

Even since earliest times, when the amount of forest was far greater than it is now, people have felt the need to plant trees. This, in essence, is a recognition of the significance of place and the quality which particular species of tree could contribute to specific locations. Tree planting has been one of the archetypal activities which people have engaged in since before recorded history. Indeed, recorded history often seems to have ignored the practice of tree planting, probably because it has not fitted into any convenient category. I am not referring to planting trees as a 'crop' for coppicing or timber production, but to what has become known as "amenity planting", though "amenity" must be interpreted in a much wider way than usual.

Trees are living beings - they grow, mature and decay. It is therefore in the nature of things that we cannot always be sure whether particular trees or groups of trees were artificially planted or grew up naturally. Indeed, this distinction itself can be blurred as many trees, naturally regenerated, have been protected and tended over many years, thus encouraging their growth. And planted trees can have a magic all of their own.

The concept of trees as landmarks first entered my consciousness after meeting Tony Wedd in 1961. He had been looking at clumps of Scots pines in the landscape around his home on the Kent/Sussex border, in connection with an idea he had about the link between unexplained aerial phenomena and prominent sites in the landscape, which he expounded in his booklet "*Skyways and Landmarks*".[116,49]

These clumps of Scots pines, on the ridges of the hills surrounding his home in Chiddingstone, were marvellous places - visible from afar, poking up above the skyline. They were, however, surprisingly difficult to get to, as one had to battle in some cases through heavy undergrowth. But, once standing in the midst of the tall pines, the atmosphere was magical and could be strongly felt. There was a certain peace

between the pines, and an uplifting of the spirit so that you knew that it was a special place. The quotation from A.A. Milne with which I start this chapter gives some idea of this feeling, and in fact describes one of the most prominent clumps which Tony Wedd investigated - Gill's Lap.

The attribution of significance to clumps of trees in the landscape, primarily Scots pine, dates back to the 1920s, when the antiquarian, Alfred Watkins, noticed that they frequently fell on the old straight tracks which he had recently discovered in Herefordshire and the Welsh border areas and which he called 'leys'. He postulated that the old tracks were marked by a variety of indicators, including trees and tree-clumps, particularly Scots pine.[115]

Watkins became convinced that the people who had originally laid out the tracks had chosen Scots pine as landmarks because they were very rare in the Welsh border counties and their presence would be an indication to the traveller that they had been planted deliberately.

But how can we identify whether a clump had been planted deliberately? Firstly, it will tend to be in a prominent position, so as to be visible from a long way off. They are often sited on the side or flank of a hill rather than on the very top. This gives maximum visibility from the widest area, being sufficiently near the top to be seen from quite a distance, but capable of being seen from the valley immediately below the hill, and by someone climbing up its side.

Also, close examination will reveal that it is a true "clump" rather than a line, such as might mark a hedge or a scatter which has spread naturally. The clump will tend to retain its form, which is roughly circular, and will be compact. It may be contained by some sort of earthwork on all sides, although this may not be particularly pronounced.

It has been noted by writers such as Nigel Pennick, Ian Taylor and Brian Richardson that trees in a clump or group seem to operate as one entity rather than just as individuals, and that this is most evident in terms of the shape which the overall clump takes on. As Pennick says:

> *"Tree clumps often have the form of a unified overall canopy, making the whole wood look like a single massive tree."*[92]

My friend, Brian Richardson, calls this an archetypal shape and suggests that it seems to be evidence of a group organism:

> *"I didn't stop and ask 'Why would it be that the trees at one end of a clump are smaller than the ones in the middle?' I just noticed it and wondered if that were the case. And then, just the other week, I was out on my bike, cycling over the Lincolnshire Wolds, when I saw another grove of trees, and the wind was blowing, and I realised: 'That's it!!!' It's for the purpose of streamlining, decreasing wind resistance. That way the whole grove of trees benefits.'"*[100]

Then again, clumps will have trees and shrubs which are in some way distinctive in the locality. With Scots pines, this is usually due to their height, towering above the other trees, and the colour of their foliage, being much darker. They are also, of course, evergreen, and would stand out even more strongly in winter. Other trees were also chosen, however, and this is where it is difficult to define precise rules: one has to rely on intuition when visiting the sites.

Watkins quoted some striking examples of Scots pine clumps in and around his native Herefordshire, and I vividly remember visiting one, called Cole's Tump, near Orcop, in the mid 1960s. But trees are living beings: they grow, mature and, in time, die back into the earth from which they were born. And tree clumps change, as I saw with Cole's Tump when I went back to visit it in the 1960s and again in the 1980s. It was no longer the thriving clump it was in Watkins' day. The trees were dying and not being replaced. In another 50 years, unless something is done, Cole's Tump will be no more. And Gill's Lap suffered greatly in the hurricane of October 1987, as did many other prominent clumps, such as Chanctonbury Ring on the South Downs in Sussex.

Now, Watkins and Wedd were claiming that some of the clumps that they had identified dated back several thousand years to prehistoric times when the old straight tracks may have been laid out. But if some of these clumps have disappeared, even in the years that I have been studying them, how likely is it that they date back to prehistoric times? Of course, they wouldn't be the same trees, and if there had been spontaneous regeneration on the same site, helped by local people who realised their significance, then they could have survived to the present day. Indeed, it may only have been the disruptions to rural traditions that have taken place this century and our own lack of awareness that have accelerated the decline.

But just as landscapes are constantly changing there are also changes in how we see the old straight tracks and their markers. It is now being realised that they are not the remnants of an ancient system of communication which covered the country, but the influence of what we might call 'the linear archetype' on people's perception of the landscape. We are almost certainly looking at stretches of straight track, perhaps church or coffin paths, which date back a few hundred years at most and not a few thousand. Ultimately this doesn't really matter: it frees us from any necessity to view tree clumps as originating in prehistoric times and enables us to see them as they are - prominent marks at significant points, probably planted in the last 200 or 300 years, for a variety of purposes.

Watkins was, however, a good observer of the landscape and, whatever ultimately becomes of his ideas about leys, he certainly noticed the frequency with which Scots pines, as individuals or as clumps, were situated at prominent points in the landscape beside ancient tracks. Indeed, there is now much evidence to suggest that because of their distinctive qualities Scots pines were planted in clumps to mark drove roads in the Welsh border country, in Wiltshire and elsewhere, to indicate a welcome, hospitality for the drovers and grazing for the cattle and sheep.[69]

Before these present days when people (or rather insurance companies) are worried about the presence of a tree close to a house, in case it undermined the foundations, it was very much a tradition in many places to plant a tree adjacent to the front door, ostensibly to provide protection.

The rowan is typical in this respect, being traditionally planted to ward off witches. In fact, the opposite is true. Witches used to plant them to indicate a "safe house". Similarly, in Oxfordshire in more recent times, Scots pines were planted outside houses to indicate that the inhabitants were Jacobite supporters.[69]

That other native evergreen, the yew, also seems to have been used as a waymark and to indicate boundaries, as Andrew Morton recounts with regard to Shropshire:

> *"Throughout the county can be found remnant lines of yew trees that mark old routes and boundaries across the countryside. These 'marker' trees are often to be found leading towards parish churches and chapels.*
>
> *There are also yews found growing alone in fields. Either these trees have been left because of the superstition that to fell a yew brings misfortune, or because the trees formed part of a 'marking' system now lost or destroyed.*

The dark foliage of the yew is easy to pick out in the landscape. In the Summer the crown is darker than all other trees and in the Winter the evergreen appearance is easily distinguished from long distances. Even today people occasionally use these trees as 'guiding points' or landmarks on walks. In times when all country folk attended Sunday church services, many coming on foot, the yews must have been valuable 'signposts'."[87]

Morton also mentions the practice of planting landmark yews in other parts of the country, including those flanking the Pilgrims' Way between Winchester and Canterbury, of which Julia Cartwright says:

"Certain peculiarities, it is interesting to notice, mark its course from beginning to end. It clings to the hills, and wherever it is possible, avoids the marshy ground of the valleys. It runs, not on the summit of the downs, but about half-way down the hillside, where there is shelter from the wind, as well as sunshine to be had under the crest of the ridge. And its course is marked by rows of yew-trees, often remarkable for their size and antiquity. Some of these are at least seven or eight hundred years old, and must have reared their ancient boughs on the hillside before the feet of pilgrims ever trod these paths. So striking is this feature of the road, and so fixed is the idea that some connection exists between these yew trees and the Pilgrims' Way, that they are often said to have been planted with the express object of guiding travellers along the road to Canterbury. This, however, we need hardly say, is a fallacy. Yews are by no means peculiar to the Pilgrims' Way, but are to be found along every road in chalk districts. They spring up in every old hedgerow on this soil, and are for the most part sown by the birds. But the presence of these venerable and picturesque forms does lend an undeniable charm to the ancient track. And in some places where the line of cultivation gradually spreading upwards has blotted out every other trace of

the road, where the ploughshare has upturned the sod, and the hedgerows have disappeared, three or four of these grand old trees may still be seen standing by themselves, in the midst of a ploughed field, the last relics of a bygone age."[21]

In my book *"Secret Places of the Goddess"*[50], I refer to the way in which I, and many others, could be drawn towards certain spots or locations in the landscape which "felt special". I did not attempt to define any more precisely what that "feeling special" consisted of, since most of those I have talked to about it have said something like: "Yes, I've had those experiences, too!" But certainly trees feature sufficiently often to suggest that they had an important contribution to make to the "special feeling" of a place, as if they were necessary to "complete" a place in some way. I felt that perhaps this may have something to do with the balance of elements, trees contributing the quality of air to a site. Certainly many of the clumps of Scots Pines and, perhaps even more so, the solitary pines, perhaps survivors of earlier clumps, or perhaps always on their own, are in places which have a certain "feel" about them - places that are already special in some way. This is nearly always accompanied by the feeling that they make the site more special, and can provide a focus, as generations of landscape painters have demonstrated. Sutton Palmer's painting of the Eden Valley, which I mentioned in Chapter 4, is just one example of this.

Now, these trees may well have seeded naturally, finding the right conditions to flourish. This would include the right soil and micro-climate, protection from predators, including the human needs for agriculture and other activity, and, perhaps especially, the right subtle energy environment. Indeed, despite the indicators I have already mentioned, it is in practice difficult to tell whether a clump or an individual tree is self-seeded or deliberately planted, and ultimately this does not really matter. There was, however, a fashion from the 17th Century up to the present-day for landowners to plant trees at prominent sites, possibly in imitation of the landscaping of such designers as Capability Brown and Humphrey Repton, but on a much smaller scale.

We really know very little about the creation of landmarks by tree planting, mainly because little was written down by the farmers and landowners who planted them. It is clear, however, that they were close to the land and knew instinctively its every detail and the spirit of the landscape which dwelt there. They planted where they felt it right to do so, and we now have as a legacy the presence of trees in the landscape which can help to reveal its hidden nature. In essence, it doesn't matter how old a feature is. It's what it's like now that counts, for the magic of the Earth quickly imbues a place with special quality. And certainly there often seems to have been an instinctive awareness of landscape aesthetics, where the planting of trees has increased the significance and attractiveness of a specific location.

Chapter 10

Sacred Groves

"Even the smallest woods have their secrets and secret places, their unmarked precincts, and I am certain all sacred buildings, from the greatest cathedral to the smallest chapel, and in all religions, derive from the natural aura of certain woodland or forest settings."

John Fowles - *The Tree*

To anyone who has felt the emotional effect of being amongst trees, the words "Sacred Grove" conjure up a variety of images, but particularly that of a special place created by the form of the trees themselves which was recognised by people in the past who frequented it for rituals.

Yet for all the talk about sacred groves, we really know very little about them. Where were they, and do any still exist? What were they like? Who went there, and for what purposes?

When any one of these questions is posed, a mist comes down through which only glimpses can be seen. Yet the image of the sacred grove remains strangely attractive, as if we instinctively know what they are and could recognise one, or the remains of one, if we were to see it.

The one thing we think we know about sacred groves is that they were associated with the Druids. Place name evidence provides a clue, as Angela Blaen makes clear:

> "... consider the meaning of the word nymet, or nimet, which is related to Gaulish nemeton (holy place), Welsh nyfed and Old Welsh nimet (a shrine or holy place), Old Saxon nimid (a forest sanctuary or holy grove) and Celtic nemeto-, nemitis (a holy place. Jacob Grimm related nimid to the Latin nemus (a sacred grove), and C.E. Stevens noted that:
>
> "In Ireland ... the word nemed, occasionally found in a pagan context, is, in Irish literature, not uncommon in the sense of holy place, sanctuary, church"."[12]

The Ravenna Cosmography, written in 600 C.E., gives a list of sacred groves, each with the 'nemet' element in their names. Craig Chapman gives details of the locations of and historical references to several of these, and describes such a grove as follows:

> "... a sacred grove could well have been enclosed by a simple bank and ditch separating the sacred land from the well cultivated, acculturated landscape outside. Woodbanks mentioned in the 12th century seem mostly to have been already in existence, relics of the Anglo-Saxon or Norse landscape, even possibly dating back to the Iron Age ... for the circular woodbanks of the Celts differed little if any from those of later woodcrafters."[22]

This is a very different 'feel' to the archetypal image of the sacred grove which most of us have, as Chapman himself admits:

> "The classical writers imagined a wilder grove within the imagination, in which Druids celebrated barbaric rites; some believed the Druids retreated under Roman

*oppression from open air gatherings to closet themselves
and their dark rites in the remnants of the wild-wood,
away from civilisation ..."*[22]

Natural Origins

I want to rescue that archetypal image from the limited
context in which the words 'sacred grove' have been used
above, and free them to mean any group of trees or location
which was considered particularly sacred in ancient times
(without necessarily specifying how ancient) and where rituals
in some form were regularly carried out. As we have seen, the
circular form occurs naturally over time if a yew is allowed to
grow without interference so that its branches take root as the
central bole decays. Alan Bleakley also comments:

> *"In forest and woodland, oak, yew, lime, and elm in
> particular often form perfect circles, or rings, of trees, by
> putting up new shoots from suckers ..."*[16]

Pines will also frequently grow in a circular form, as in many
of the clumps mentioned in the previous chapter.

In ancient times, circular formations in nature were
considered sacred, and places where they occurred were
therefore similarly felt to be sacred in their own right. The
fairy rings formed by certain fungi, the mating paths of the
roe deer, flowers and fungi growing round the site of a former
tree, not to mention crop circles - all may have provided the
inspiration for the establishment of a sacred grove. If we use
the term 'sacred grove' in this wider sense, they may have
been recognised or planted in any century from ancient times
to the present day. Apart from the ancient yew, oak and beech
groves, Tony Wedd has made a link between the Celtic sacred
trees and the presence of a sacred grove. Describing a tree
clump in Wiltshire, he says:

"The clump is mostly of beech, but also carries Ash, Elm, Elder, Yew, Box, Hornbeam, Holly, Ivy, Sycamore, Privet, May and Willow. I fancy it is an old Celtic Grove, planted with the 13 trees of the tree calendar, which were also the names of the Beth-Luis-Nion alphabet letters"[117]

How the Sacred Groves became the Churchyards

If, for convenience, we use 'grove' in this wider sense, it is clear that we are looking at a far greater number of places than have been identified in the historical documents referred to by Chapman and others. Using my definition, every community would not only be within reach of at least one sacred grove, but might very well be centred on it.

How might we find such groves? One way might be to look at the historical evidence. To start with, we have the very interesting written records of the early Christianisation of this country. Pope Gregory, writing to Archbishop Mellitus in 601CE states:

"I have come to the conclusion that the temples of the idols in England should not on any account be destroyed. Augustine must smash the idols, but the temples themselves should be sprinkled with holy water and altars set up in them in which relics are to be enclosed ... I hope the people (seeing their temples are not destroyed) will leave their idolatry and yet continue to frequent the places as formerly, so coming to know and revere the true God."

In other words, for the sacred sites of the ancient peoples, we could do worse than look at where some of our long-established churches are situated.

The other important factor, as we have seen from the work of Allen Meredith, is that yew trees are now generally considered to be much older than was previously thought. We now know that yews at any rate live long enough to have been around at the same time as the Druids, and there is, for example, a yew grove near Salisbury called Great Yews, where Marion Davies has drawn attention to "the long avenues leading to a circle of grass" which she feels may be the remains of a druidical grove.[32] It has also been demonstrated that some churchyard yews are actually considerably older than the church itself.

Putting these two facts together - that, at least in some cases, the churches were located on the old pagan sacred sites and that many of the churchyard yew trees were older than the churches - we come to the conclusion that many of the ancient churchyards are, in fact, sacred groves and that the older yew trees the remnants of those that were found there. As Morton confirms, both the groves and the older churchyards were mostly circular:

> *"Ancient religious sites, based upon the magic cult are ... invariably round. Within is the sacred, without is the profane. The circles were constructed by various means ... and were demarcated by evergreen trees, in Britain normally the yew. ... The fringing of sacred sites by planted trees is reminiscent of the sacred grove which was presumably achieved by felling and clearance or occurred naturally"[87]*

Also writing about churchyards, Alan Mitchell comments:

> *"... the trees were there long before the Saxon church and Norman rebuilds. They were on holy ground, the tribal elders' meeting places and the churches were built near them to take over the holy site and also to gain good shelter for their porches from wind and snow."[85]*

210

In terms of the age of many of the trees, this sheds some doubt on the traditional idea that yews were planted in churchyards to provide material for making bows. What really seems to have happened is that people, probably over many generations, became aware of natural yew groves, whereby a circular space surrounded by a ring of yews had been created naturally by the rooting of the dipping branches and the eventual decay of the original central trunk. They could sense the atmosphere and probably experienced certain things there which gave it sacred significance. Rituals would naturally take place there and, when Christianity had become a sufficiently dominant force, the site would be taken over and a church built in the centre.

Probably by then most of the yews would have decayed, as Allen Meredith found that Saxon churches were often located so that the surviving yews provided protection for the entrance porch.

At this stage, the transformation to the churchyard that we know today would be almost complete. A wall may have been built around it, burials (which may have been a feature of the old groves) were carried out within the bounds of the churchyard, and additional yews and other trees were often planted, carrying on a very old tradition. Even today, many churchyards are wild life refuges. There is no real way of knowing if a churchyard was originally a sacred grove, but if there was known to be a church in Saxon times, and if the churchyard is circular, it is a good indication.

Of course, sacred groves are in other places besides churchyards, dating from many different periods, and the best way to find them is to get to know a stretch of countryside as well as you can and then let your intuition guide you. I am sure that many of the clumps and solitary trees which I refer to in the last chapter are on the sites of sacred groves. Ultimately, the feel of the place - the atmosphere - is as good a guide as any.

Bringing the Trees Indoors

I suspect that the sacred groves in the way I have defined them were open-air affairs, and accorded to the old wisdom that to worship the God and the Goddess one must go out to their realms.

With the building of the churches, however, people felt they needed to bring the trees indoors with them. Sometimes this was done literally, as with the modern-day Christmas tree, but more usually it was symbolic. We have already looked at the wealth of tree symbolism in churches in Chapter 4 - the Green Man, Tree of Life, etc. - but in fact the very buildings themselves were reminders of the sacred grove, as Morton says:

> "In the Christian Old Testament, the conflict is evident between the limited monotheistic god and the multiple gods that grew in every forest or grove. The history of the Christian (Catholic) church is rife with the destruction of sacred groves and the older Earth religions and the construction of monasteries and churches upon those holy sites. However, when the new churches and temples were built, symbols of the trees were included in the decorations within them, and their veneration still was evident in subtle ways. ... The pillars of Greek temples were probably representations of tree trunks in that they have stylised foliage at the top. It is thought that the Greek temple is a formalised architectural version of the sacred grove. ... It is hard not to see in the mediaeval churches and cathedrals the resemblance to the yew in the characteristic fluting and spreading pillars."[87]

Sacred Groves Today

Whether the grove is essentially natural or artificial is really only a secondary consideration. Indeed, ultimately, it is our recognition of a group of trees as a sacred grove which becomes the determining factor in its definition, and it is undoubtedly true that places can become sacred through use.

At some stage, the qualities of such a place were recognised and a certain amount of planting or what I call 'tending' may have taken place, much planted following various occult and Druid revivals of the 17th, 18th and 19th centuries which may now have attained a striking "presence".

Sacred groves are still used today for the performance of ritual, and I have been to many myself for such purposes. Particularly where it is an old site, there often seems to be a strong feeling that similar rituals have taken place in the past and that the power has been built up gradually over a long period of time. These sites usually seem to have mature trees and one can often sense the remnants of a grove which had fallen into decay through lack of care. But not always! Some sites are still cared for and one of the strongest ways in which a site can be loved, as well as by practical action, is the performance of a ritual.

Indeed, sacred groves can be created today. The essence is to recognise what is already there. It may not ever have been used for ritual in the past, but if you recognise the qualities of the place, that is the first and vital step. Try to appreciate the sense of space that is there and how it is defined by the trees and landforms. Acknowledge the main trees - there may be one in the centre of the grove, or one at each of the four quarters, or in a circle around a central open area. Find the boundaries of the grove and the right way to approach it. Above all, get to know it well and, with the permission of the spirit of the place, perform rituals there. Be guided by the place rather than by anything you have read (including these words) and you will know that you are doing the right thing.

Ros Briagha tells of one sacred grove which was created at the pagan community at Elfane:

"About ten years ago, my partner and I moved up to a little small-holding in Wales, with our focus being to create a safe pagan space for ceremony and worship for ourselves and others. We started by constructing a large fire-pit and then piled up turf slabs and stones to make a three-foot high circular bank around the fire, and we levelled the land inside.

The finished ring is about forty feet in diameter, with an inner circle capable of accommodating over forty people, and yet not seeming empty with just a few. The fire pit is about four feet wide and two feet high. At each of the cardinal points there is a stone, between one and two feet high, and a big one supported by two yew pillars at the North as an altar. The finishing touches are the trees. These are based on one of the variations of the Celtic tree calendar, though over the years it has developed in its own unique way."[17]

Willow, hawthorn, oak, holly, magnolia, apple, blackthorn, elder, yew, birch, rowan, ash and alder were planted around the circle. The article from which I took the above account appeared in 1990, so the trees should have matured considerably by now.

Of course, there are many ways to approach the creation of a sacred grove, and this is just one example. Others are now appearing in many parts of the country, keeping alive the old tradition of the sacred grove.

Chapter 11

Tree Magic and Ritual

"Our delight in what we make from natural materials is a natural extension of our delight in nature itself."
Kim Taplin - *Tongues in Trees*

The word 'ritual' often conjures up some elaborate ceremony, with robes, incense and candles. Whilst this might sometimes be an accurate picture, ritual in its essence is actually something very much more simple. Each time we stop and acknowledge the beauty of a view in the countryside we are engaging in ritual. Each time we take a drink from a holy well and feel gratitude for its presence we are engaging in ritual. And each time we stop and reach out to touch a tree during a walk through the woods, feeling its bark beneath our fingers and experiencing a sensation of calm we are engaging in a form of ritual. In other words, ritual is anything that we do with awareness of the deeper, spiritual dimensions to life.

When it comes to trees, one of the simplest of all rituals and something that we do instinctively is to hug them. It seems almost archetypal in nature, and we are reminded of the Salabhanjia customs that we looked at in Chapter 3. This account by Claire Bellenis will serve as an example:

> *"The first time I actually hugged a tree was in Yosemite Park in the States. On a group nature walk, our guide,*

*who was a huge, beefy ranger, called the group together
and asked each person to choose a tree, go up to it and
give it a big hug. He told us (to much laughter from the
group) that he did this every day and that he formed
relationships with the various trees. As he was so
obviously big and butch, the ridicule which a smaller
man would have been subjected to from some members of
the group was spared him.*

*Anyway, we all dutifully trotted off and hugged our
chosen tree, and it was a revelation. I felt a great surge of
energy and love coming from the trunk right into and
through me, and I have been hugging trees and chatting
to them ever since."*[11]

I have found that one of the ways of drawing people and trees
closer together is to hold hands around a particularly large
tree, where the trunk may need three, four or even more
people to encircle it. This provides a powerful circuit if kept up
for a few minutes, where energy is circulated along the arms
of those present and between them, the tree and the earth
beneath.

The Ritual Site

Trees are often the setting for outdoor rituals and it is almost
as if they are a substitute for the shelter in which we normally
reside. We tend to feel uncomfortable in the middle of the wide
open spaces and would prefer our 'backs to the wall', possibly
unconsciously dating back to the time when we might literally
be 'stabbed in the back'. In other words, seen in terms of
Prospect/Refuge theory, they are a refuge.

This possibly explains the attraction which trees and woods
have for us, as they provide plenty of opportunities for us to
see without being seen, such as Lorenz' example of the edge of
a wood, where one can see out clearly but, because of the low

light conditions, no-one outside the wood can see you. And the image of Robin Hood hiding in the foliage of an oak tree ready to drop on some unsuspecting traveller passing beneath remains vivid in my mind from what must have been repeated occurrences of the same incident on television programmes of 40 years ago.

And so it tends to be with rituals - we want to be in nature, but enfolded in her arms - and those arms are the trees. Woods and forests provide this enfoldment in abundance and also that protection and secrecy which a vulnerable and persecuted minority, such as the followers of the Old Religion, would welcome. John Fowles' example of the Devon and Dorset Independents which I quote in Chapter 8 is another example.

Indeed, the wood is more than just the setting for our ritual: it is an active participant. This may involve procession along ancient pathways in the mode of walking meditation, or even the uninhibited exuberance of the Wild Hunt, as Doreen Valiente remembers:

> "It was a full moon Esbat of about half a dozen people. We made our invocation, drank a toast to the Old Gods, and then danced in a circle. By the time the rite ended, we were all merry and exhilarated. It was a mild, clear night, with a silver moon shining through the trees. Somehow, instead of dispersing quietly, we continued to dance through the woods. I had brought along an old hunting horn, which the leader borrowed, and at the sound of this we laughed, leaped, shrilled the old cries and ran down the path between the trees, still attired in our hooded cloaks. Eventually, we came to a breathless halt at the edge of the woods, where lighted roads and civilization began. We looked at each other, and the leader said to us, 'You know what we've been doing? We've been playing the Wild hunt!'

We realized that he was right. Some atavistic impulse seemed to have taken hold of us. It was a strange, uncanny experience, and one that I shall never forget."[111]

Trees naturally seem to want to join in the ritual. Many is the time when I have been out searching for a site suitable for a particular ritual. I have found the general location, perhaps a wood or common, and I am homing in on the actual site. Usually, in such a situation, I find that a tree enters my consciousness with particular strength and an area of ground adjacent to it suggests itself as the ritual location. It is quite possible for a tree to be the centre of a circle but more usually, at least in my experience, it is on the edge of the ritual site.

Here, I must draw attention to the importance which pagans attach to the magic circle and the four quarters. These are the primary directions - North, East, South and West. They emphasise the position of the circle as being "between the worlds" - fixing it in relation to both the earth and the heavens. These four cardinal points are usually marked around the perimeter of the circle, perhaps by candles or other ritual objects.

I have, however, noticed that, very naturally, trees seem to position themselves around the edge of the circle at points corresponding to the primary directions, without appearing to move at all! What I think is actually happening is that ritual space is chosen, at an unconscious level, in a way which harmonises with the natural spacing of the trees - a process which is easier to do than to describe.

Certainly one tree usually stands out as being particularly significant and it is usually at its foot and among its roots, particularly if it is a beech, that the altar cloth is laid, with ritual tools set out upon it.

Many trees seem to be natural altars - not as smooth and level as the front-room coffee-table, perhaps, but a lot more powerful. The key is not to have preconceived opinions about altar layout that are too rigid to adapt to what seems right in the circumstances. In other words, we must respond willingly to the tree, seeing in its various forms opportunities rather than difficulties.

Trees with roots that come to the surface or which branch out low down near the ground provide lodging-places for lanterns or candles in jars, chalice, athame or whatever. Most trees have nooks and crannies or protrusions where suitable offerings can be left. Some even have hollows where rainwater has collected: this is especially magical and would naturally form a part of any ritual.

The altar tree may be at any of the four points of the compass. They each have their own quality and something to teach us, and it seems right to follow what the land is trying to tell us rather than adhere to some rigid doctrine which insists that the altar has to be in the north, east or wherever.

The trees provide physical markers for the magical circle, containing it and, in their branches which meet above our heads and their roots beneath our feet, echoing by their form the sphere of energy which the circle truly is.

Protection and secrecy may entail the necessity for a strong physical barrier around the ritual site. This can be characterised as the "impenetrable thicket" formed of such trees as hawthorn, blackthorn or holly, as we saw in Chapter 8 in the extract from "The Herb of Grace".

Ritual sites and trees seem to go together naturally. So it is to be expected that in our dreams, pathworkings and creations on the mental plane we come upon ritual sites which have trees as an essential element. Let me take you to one of my own. This is in a hidden, secret valley, within which is a small, steeply-sided hill. At the top is a level space large enough to act as a ritual site. Surrounding it, at the four cardinal points, are four tall trees - a beech in the east, an oak in the south, an ash in the west, and a pine in the north. Surrounding them, like a continuous protective belt, apart from a secret and sinuous passageway through at the north-east quarter, is a thicket of holly, blackthorn, hawthorn and hazel. On the ground between the trees is a carpet of pure grass.

If there are trees at the four quarters they will naturally be brought in to the ritual to represent the spirits of each direction - physical guardians, as it were, embodying that which lies beyond physical form. It often seems to happen, as a ritual proceeds, that the nature spirits of the area become curious and hover around the perimeter of the circle, usually a little way off, appearing as a misty haze. Usually there is a feeling of welcome and support, which is most encouraging.

The trees also seem to 'come alive' in a way that is not usually so obvious in ordinary reality. It is as if the casting of the circle and their inclusion on its perimeter has enabled us to approach their 'wavelength' more easily.

The energy of the circle is built up by our own joint efforts in raising power by whatever means we use; but I have the distinct feeling that the trees have a hand (or branch) in this as well, so that raising the cone of power among trees actually gives it a quality that it would otherwise not possess - perhaps like the difference between organic and artificial produce?

If we bring garlands of seasonal flowers, leaves and fruits to a ritual, it is natural to want to leave them for the Goddess, and leaving them at the foot of the trunk, or placed in the branches, often feels right.

Magical Tools

From the first time that someone picked up a stick from the forest floor to nourish a fire, people have used trees and their products: even today much of our life is bound up with them. Indeed, the very paper of the book you are now reading is almost certainly derived ultimately from a living tree.

This use of the natural products of the earth should be a joy, as the quotation by Kim Taplin with which I started this chapter reminds us. Properly used, with respect, it seems as if this joy is reciprocated, as we have seen in Dorothy Maclean's Deva communications. Indeed, it seems that our attitude to trees is the determining factor in how willing they are to give of their bounty. Trees do grow and can replace limbs which are removed. Indeed, the whole craft of coppicing is based on this principle. Clearly, respect and knowledge are important so that more is not taken than can be replaced, to ensure the healthy survival of the tree.

Dusty Miller[80] makes an interesting distinction between Deadwood, Greenwood and LiveWood.

Deadwood is, as its name suggests, wood that is no longer living. It has either fallen from the tree or is attached to it but no longer has any life force flowing through it. Deadwood is used for fuel and has certain other uses but is generally not much use for magical purposes. It has a vital role, however, in ensuring the nutrition of the soil of the forest floor as it decays back into the earth. It is therefore important to ensure that the forest is not denuded of deadwood to fuel your ritual fires and that sufficient is left to perform its natural function.

Greenwood, as defined by Miller, is 'wood stolen from the tree by force', i.e. wood taken without regard to the indwelling spirit of the tree or the tree's essential wellbeing. He explains that in such a situation of threat the tree spirit will withdraw temporarily from the tree until the threat is passed. Thus the wood obtained, whilst useful in a practical sense, does not contain anything of the tree spirit itself and thus is of lesser use for magical purposes.

By contrast, LiveWood, when taken from the tree, still retains the life force, personified as a Dryad, and can therefore be used for magical purposes. It is clear that Dusty Miller has special techniques for ensuring that the life force is retained in the wood removed from the tree, for he says:

"By using the sacred methods, rites and rituals laid down by the ancient woodcraft lore of the Old Religion, we have been able to talk with our Sacred Trees and achieve a very high degree of success."[80]

He also says, however, that:

"Every LiveWood Dryad always has a strong character of its own and no guarantee of its cooperation can be given. They will only work with the people they like and can trust. It will, therefore, pay you to take the time to make friends with them first, before requesting their help. The more you win their confidence, the more help they will give you. Treat them like a friend and they will give you a lifetime of devoted service."[80]

We see several themes implicit in this advice - the need to attune to the tree, to ask permission and to be guided as to which parts of the tree can be taken. This wise advice can also be applied to the care and use of any magical tool taken from the living tree - the need to respect the life force within and to build up your relationship with it, through respectful use, over a period of time. This is not the place to examine in detail the variety of magical tools and materials that can be obtained from trees, but listing of even the most commonly used would have to include sticks and staffs, stangs, wands, besoms, garlands and incense.

There are actually four different ways that one can acquire magical tools - making them, buying them, being given them and finding them - and we are concerned here primarily with the first way. To make a magical tool means, initially, to come upon the raw material - in the present context the branch or other part of a tree. Following, and elaborating on, Dusty Miller's advice, we might have to go through the following stages:

[1] Be clear about what you want and why you want it. This helps to build up in your mind a strong and detailed picture of the wand or stang, for example, that you wish to acquire.

[2] Be sensitive to the tides of life and to the changing seasons. Magical tools only appear at a time when you really need them. To force the situation at any other time just won't work and will result in something which will tend to work against your will rather than augmenting it.

[3] When the time is right, you will be led to the right tree. You will certainly recognise it when you come upon it and you will also recognise the branch or whatever that you are meant to take.

[4] Attune to the tree, using the way which was outlined in Chapter 5, or whatever method works for you. Take as much time as you need over this stage.

[5] Ask the tree's permission to take what you need, and then listen to the answer. If you have been through the preliminary processes and approached the tree in the right way, then the answer will very likely be "go ahead". But, do take note - this is not just a meaningless empty ritual - it means something.

[6] Make sure that you have an appropriate knife, saw, secateurs or whatever, to remove the wood cleanly, and look at the "pruning" section in gardening books to ensure that you know how to make the cut. In fact, surprisingly frequently, the branch or shoot selected will come away very easily indeed. Somehow, if it is right for you, the tree will make it as easy as possible for you to remove it without damage.

[7] Give thanks to the tree, and treat the wood you have taken with respect.

Particular woods are used for particular purposes, based on their special magical qualities. The wand is a case in point: some traditions indicate a wide range of woods depending on the purpose for which you need it.

It is not the intention of this book to give detailed instructions on how to make various magical tools: these details are readily available elsewhere. All I am intending to convey is the (very important) stage of the process where the raw materials are obtained, for in making magical tools everything needs to be done in a magical way - with awareness.

Divination

The essence of divination is being able to 'see' into the heart of a situation - into that state where the unity of the universe is experienced directly. People who live more in accordance with the natural rhythms of life can more easily 'see' - it is a part of their nature which they acknowledge and live with. Trees can encourage that state, if we are able to lower the barriers in ways that we looked at in Chapter 5. This is essential in any successful form of tree divination but it is equally important to recognise some of the languages that the tree speaks in.

Shape and pattern have meanings and the richness of form and texture in tree roots, bark and branches are a rich ground for stimulating our psychic abilities if we allow them to do so.

Another important stimulant is simulacra. These are the faces that one can see in the bark or roots of a tree if one looks in the right way. They occur because of the similar formative processes between trees and people. In one sense, they are not objectively there - you have to use your imagination. But this is one of the ways in which the tree spirit communicates, and it would be wrong to denigrate it as just imagination.

Odin perceived the runes after spending nine days and nights hanging upside down in a windswept tree. It seems clear from this that the runes are derived from the form of twigs, branching off and crossing each other and moving about in the wind. This is one of the ways in which the tree will talk to us. Even in the most fitful wind the tree is never still - the leaves rustle and the twigs rub against each other. This is the raw material from which we may divine one facet of the truth. We must, of course, first still our mind, for we are using a deeper part of ourselves for this divination.

Essentially, what is necessary is that the mind must be by-passed so that the instinctive parts of ourselves can interpret in the movements of the leaves and twigs the answers to whatever questions are posed. It is the same with the sound of the wind in the leaves - we must understand this music with other than our everyday analytical mind. We need to open up that part of us that can respond directly to movement, shape and sound. In other words, we must become engaged in shamanic practices.

Trees are the basis and inspiration for a range of divinatory systems and we have already looked at dowsing for water and other things using the forked hazel rod. Marian Green[43] describes a system which involves cutting short sticks from about twenty native trees, being careful to mark which is which because some can look very similar! The twigs, kept in a box or tube, would be thrown onto a cloth and interpreted according to their position and relationship to each other. She gives brief interpretations of the meaning of each tree, which correspond in their main outline with those which I give in Chapter 6.

Although currently difficult to get hold of, *"The Celtic Tree Oracle"*, produced by Liz and Colin Murray, is a set of cards, one for each tree of the Celtic Tree Alphabet, which can be used in a similar way to Tarot cards, with various spreads and corresponding meanings.[88]

A set of tree cards, using the illustrations by Lesley Wilkinson which appear in this book, is in course of preparation.

In this chapter we have looked at magical tools, divinatory techniques and ritual sites. The link between them is our relationship with the trees and how we can use this positively through a variety of ritual activities.

228

Chapter 12

Tree Healing

"Branches, flowers, or fruit removed from sacred trees continued to carry the holiness and sanctity of the tree within."
Pattalee Glass-Koentop - *Year of Moons; Season of Trees*

Implicit in much of this book is that trees have a healing quality that we can benefit from if we choose to do so. Even walking through a wood or standing up against the trunk of a tree will help. Indeed, healing is by far the most common form of tree magic and merits a chapter to itself for that reason alone. Trees can heal the mind and spirit as well as the body and there is clearly a link between the artistic and spiritual inspiration that trees provide and their role as healers.

Healing in the orthodox modern context does not depend on place, except in the sense that clinics, surgeries, hospitals and the like have the facilities which are necessary for the orthodox healing processes to be carried out. Even alternative or complementary therapies can be carried out virtually anywhere. In contrast, much healing in the ancient world was based on place and it was necessary to go to the place to be healed. We have the vestiges of this approach in the spa towns which reached their peak of popularity in the early 19th Century, and the places of pilgrimage such as Lourdes, where miracles are reported to occur and attract multitudes as a result.

The old practices of 'dream incubation' or 'the temple sleep', as carried out in ancient Greece, are another example of this place-related healing. It usually centred around a special spring, sacred grove or rock outcrop. The one who wanted help would settle down to sleep, as close as possible to the holy waters, sacred tree or whatever. The assistant, or 'therapeute', would wake the sleeper when they were dreaming (presumably indicated, as it is today, by rapid eye movements) and get the dreamer to recount what they were dreaming about. These dreams usually had some prophetic or divinatory content or involved contact with spirit entities, all of which could help in the healing processes.

Landscape Therapy

This concept of place-related healing, or what I call 'landscape therapy', has specific benefits and its revival would do much, not just for our own health, but for the relationship between person and landscape. In essence, it is simple. A person who requires healing is taken to a location in the landscape which provides what is needed to meet and heal their specific condition. This involves all the senses and all the elements, and trees are likely to take an important part.

What is actually happening is that the individual is being placed in a position where they can open up to the energies of the place, and the place and time is chosen to provide the energies that are needed.

In Chapter 6, some attempt was made to portray some of the main themes making up the 'personality' of various trees. A good healer should be able to gain an insight into what trees or combinations of trees are needed to provide what is lacking in any particular individual, and this, of course, is what lies behind the use of the various tree essences, flower remedies and essential oils in aromatherapy. The difference between these and landscape therapy is that in landscape therapy the individual is taken out into a landscape which meets their specific needs.

The development of landscape therapy as a formal discipline is still in its very early stages, but we can see that what it is doing is providing a "healing atmosphere" which is specific for a particular individual. This "atmosphere" is, of course, on all levels, both physical, psychic and spiritual, and encourages entering an altered state of consciousness. It is the "atmosphere" which does the healing and the role of the therapist is to find the place that provides what that particular individual needs and to find ways in which they can benefit most from their experiences of being there. Many traditional and sacred sites, such as the sacred groves, were doing just this, and healing has always been an important part of their function.

Tree Healing through the Senses

By tree healing in the context of landscape therapy we mean the healing which occurs by coming into direct contact in some way with a tree or trees themselves. There are many facets to this and we have already implicitly examined some of these in earlier chapters. We experience healing within ourselves and, in order to provide a suitable internal environment for healing to take place, we experience the external environment with as many of our senses as we can.

Primary in this respect is feeling. Touching, hugging and sitting against a tree is one of the main ways in which the healing energy can be transferred. Typical in this respect is a tree spell which was given by "W.G." in the influential magazine 'Pentagram':

> "Trees are a good source of radiant vitality on a very low-frequency scale, and this can be drawn upon under favourable conditions. A very useful application of it is

for relief, and even cure, of many backache conditions. ...
One 'makes friends' with the tree by touching it, talking
to it, and thinking into it. Circle it nine times, either
touching it with the fingertips, or with the end of your
staff. Take up the final position North, and lean back
against the tree firmly as if in the arms of a friend
(which it is); reach your hands behind you, touching the
tree as if you were holding its hands, and say or think
slowly and deeply:

O Tree;

Strong Tree; Kind Tree:

Take thou this weakness of my back.

Give me thy strength instead.

That I may be as upright as thyself

Between the Heavens   (look up)

And the earth beneath   (look down)

Secure from storm

And blessed in every branch.

  May this be so.

After this has been repeated a number of times until a
sense of "rapport" is felt, relax quietly against the tree
and simply let it work for perhaps ten minutes or so.
Breathe slowly and deeply, thinking of nothing except
peace and tranquillity. After a little, there should be a
'pulling out' feeling in the back which varies with
individuals. When it is felt that the treatment is over,
break contact gently, thank the Nature Spirits for their
help ... This process can be repeated with a number of
trees so that one's linkage with such natural sources of
healing are thereby increased. The healing process with
trees is often slow, and 'instant cures' are not very likely.
... If practicable, it is best to work this spell with bare feet
so as to establish good earth-contact."[114]

Probably secondary in a healing sense is the scent of trees. Whilst pagans were always aware of the power of scent through the use of incenses, it is only relatively recently that aromatherapy has emphasised the connections between scent and healing. Using bottled essential oils for massage within consultation rooms, whilst valuable, is not the only way that the natural aromas, many of which are from trees, can be used. An older and more natural way is to visit the tree itself. The scents are more subtle than in the concentrated essential oils, but they are combined with the scents of other plants in the vicinity in a much more delicate way than could be done artificially. Of course, such scents will vary according to the season, time of day, and weather, but each place is unique in its combination of scents and, through breathing the atmosphere, particularly in a wood or in the vicinity of notable trees, a unique effect will result.

Pine resins are a good example. As Mirov and Hasbrouck state:

> "All of us get elated and emotional as we stroll through a pine grove on a hot summer day when the old trees fill the air with their pungent fragrance. Big bonfires made of pitchy pinewood have a peculiar mystic fascination. As we sit watching the sparks going up, and as we inhale the fragrant smoke, we are inclined to become philosophical or to sing nostalgic songs. ... Longfellow wrote beautifully of 'Piny odours in the night air.' We are all poets when we are in the pinewoods."[84]

Laurie Lee, in his account of a walk into a mountain range through the heart of Spain, gives a vivid description of this:

> "Already cool winds were blowing down from its peaks, and the plain was lifting into little hills, and by the next afternoon I'd left the wheat behind me and entered a world of Nordic pinewoods. Here I slipped off the heat like a sweat-soaked shirt and slept an hour among the

resinous trees - a fresh green smell as sweet as menthol
compared with the animal reek of the plain. I noticed
that each tree, slashed with a pattern of fishbone cuts,
was bleeding gum into little cups. The wounded trunks
seemed to be running with drops of amber, stinging the
air with their piercing scent, while some of the older
trees, bled dry and abandoned, curled in spirals like
burning paper. But it was a good place to sleep; the wood
was empty of flies, who had learnt to avoid its sticky
snares, and the afternoon sun sucked up the flavour of
each tree till the whole wood swam in incense like a
church."[60]

Sound, sight and the more subtle senses also contribute to the
creation of an 'atmosphere' in which healing can take place. I
have already quoted the passage from Thomas Hardy's *"Under
the Greenwood Tree"* which drew attention to the varying
sounds made by the wind blowing through the branches of
different trees, and I have mentioned the suggestion that wind
is the sound of trees talking to each other. If so, then we too
can surely benefit from the sound of trees talking to each
other, for they will talk to us as well if we care to listen in the
right way. It is said that some Scandinavian music has been
composed as a direct result of contact with trees, and we
might contemplate that the healing power of music might, at
its roots, have a parallel in the healing power of the wind
sounding in the trees.

The conscious siting of tree clumps and individual trees on
hilltops or the brows of hills may have at least something to do
with the ability of the wind to make the trees 'speak'. Peter
Lennon, writing about Professor John Hull, who is blind,
points out that:

> *"Trees have no existence for a blind man unless there is*
> *wind. And the sound of rain helps the darkened world*
> *come alive for him."*[61]

And Robert Graves says that "one meaning of inspiration is listening to the wind in a sacred grove".[42]

Alan Bleakley also makes the point forcefully:

> *"In the forms of the branches and the whispering, singing, shouting and crying of the trees in calmness, wind and storm, are raw, basic languages - forms and patterns"*[16]

The visual sense has a definite role in the healing process, and we may perhaps think of colour healing in this context.

In a subtle way, the perception of beauty and harmony in the natural and built environment has a definite and cumulative effect on our psychic well-being, as the crafts of landscape and townscape aesthetics imply if not specifically state. In other words, and in the specific context of this book, being in a wood or amongst trees, seeing the life force expressed in their trunks and branches, in the shape and form of their leaves, and in the way in which trees relate to each other and to the land in which they grow, affects that deep and natural part of us, which responds in recognition of something it may have long have repressed.

I noticed quite some time ago that there seemed to be some sort of correlation between a person's aesthetic appreciation of landscape and the extent to which they were free of emotional and physical blockages to the free flow of energy in their body. I explored this theme and came to the realisation that what we might call the 'life energy' in the individual was in some way recognising and responding to the same life energy in different features in the landscape and that this was experienced in aesthetic terms. I expanded on this basic idea in a series of articles entitled *"Landscape Energy and Experience"*[46] and *"Experiencing the Subtle Geography of the Earth"*[47,48].

In essence, what I think is happening when we experience the trees with as many of our senses as we can is really a kind of sympathetic magic. Coming into contact with a system (the tree) where the life energy is flowing freely encourages the flow of that same energy within ourselves, dissolving blockages and promoting health in the most natural way possible.

Sacred Water - The Essence of the Trees

To attempt to extract and take away the healing essence of the trees is a little like trying to capture the waterfall in a box. In the case of the waterfall, the water is retained but its essential quality - that of free-falling movement - is lost. This is the rationale behind what I call landscape therapy, but in the case of trees there are certain qualities that can be extracted and carried some distance.

Trees have long been known to possess qualities in their constituent parts which can help the healing process. To take just one example, hawthorn berries will regulate the heart by stimulating or depressing its activity according to what is needed to adjust to a normal functioning. This was the knowledge that the village witch possessed and which was handed down through the generations. It came of a deep understanding based on observation over many years as well as secrets imparted at the right times.

Herbalism dates back thousands of years and the properties of trees have always been prominent in any imparted body of herbal knowledge. Some are fortunate enough to be able to receive knowledge in the old way, but for most of us it is a combination of book learning and observation. One of the best books is still "*A Modern Herbal*" by Mrs. M. Grieve, first published in 1931 and still widely available.[44] The active parts of trees, which may in specific cases be the leaves, flowers or fruits, and occasionally the bark, can be used fresh, or can be dried and used as an infusion, or added to alcohol, when it becomes known as a tincture, which keeps a lot longer. The point to note is that it is the essence of the tree which is taken to the person needing healing rather than the other way around.

More recently, other methods of obtaining the essence of trees have been found, one being the extraction of the essential oils. Not all trees will yield an essential oil: it tends to be the more aromatic ones such as Juniper and Scots Pine.

The characters of the individual species of trees that we looked at in Chapter 6 are subtle qualities which reach to the most fundamental energy streams of which the universe is made up, such as strength, attraction, severity, comfort, delicacy, freshness and joy. To capture these qualities requires a subtlety of approach which homoeopathy was probably the first to recognise. This works on very subtle levels - at the level of the formative patterns which underlie physical form. Thus an immensely diluted version of a particular plant - often so diluted that it is highly unlikely that there is even a single molecule of the original ingredient left - can be very powerful in tackling deep-seated problems.

Dr. Edward Bach[8] developed a series of remedies which dealt with deep spiritual conditions. His method was to float a flower of a particular plant on pure spring water in the sunshine until the essence of the flower had been transferred to the water, which was then preserved, using an alcohol base. Many of the plants which Bach used were trees, including among others Aspen, Beech, Crab Apple, Elm, Holly, Hornbeam, Oak, Pine and Willow. A brief look at the wording in the guidance notes for the use of the Bach remedies will reveal that what are being described are existing conditions - deep conditions of the spirit undoubtedly, but conditions which the Bach remedies would be able to treat.

In recent years, other remedies and essences have begun to be made, in much the same way as the Bach ones. An example is the Bailey essences, discovered and produced by Arthur Bailey, a well-known medical dowser. He expanded the range of remedies beyond the 38 Bach ones, and focused on their use for mental conditions.

More recently, and more relevant for our present purposes, are the Green Man Tree Essences, made from the flowers of native and naturalised trees, and discovered and produced by Simon and Sue Lilly, who state:

> *"Each essence holds the vibration of a particular tree species so that, when used, the qualities of the tree become available to you to enhance your life ... Because they stimulate the subtle energy fields and the aura it is only necessary to bring the tree essences into the aura for them to start working."*[64]

> *They give various suggestions as to how the essences can be used, including adding to bathwater or massage oil, rubbing on pulse points of the body, or mixing with water and putting in a plant sprayer to spray around the room. They describe this latter as being an " ... instantaneous way of infusing the essence into your aura and like walking into a grove of your favourite trees!"*[64]

They also give details of what each essence is capable of achieving, generally expressed in far more positive terms than the Bach remedies. For example, they give the keyword "beauty" for Birch and the description given is:

> *"Ability to experience beauty and calmness. Tolerance of self and others. For those who find it difficult to express themselves."*[64]

In whatever way we care to partake of them, trees and their products can heal us because they have the qualities that can help us - calm from the rush of everyday life, the long-term perspective, a deep realisation of the cycles of life, death and rebirth, and a greater awareness of our surroundings on all levels. These qualities, and many more including the more specific ones manifested by the individual species, can trees give us if we will only let them.

Enᴅwoᴙᴅs

"I cherish trees because of their natural correspondence with greener, more mysterious processes of mind ... and because they seem to me the best, most revealing messengers to us from all nature, the nearest its heart."

John Fowles - *The Tree*

I have focused in this book on trees as living beings, with spiritual dimensions and living in community, from whom we can learn much about life if we are so inclined, and I have given hints on how to make contact with them.

We have seen that trees have qualities such as longevity, stillness and the capacity for regeneration which we can incorporate into our own lives, and yet, as we know, things are not always well between trees and people. Kim Taplin quotes The Book of Revelation: "Hurt not the earth, neither the sea, nor the trees" and comments:

> *"Today the earth is being hurt, and the sea, and the trees, on such a scale that no celebration can carry weight, ring true or have integrity if it fails to take account of it."*[107]

This has not been, at least overtly, a book about the ecological crises which are facing the Earth and of which people and trees are both inevitably a part. And yet, such crises can only be solved if each of us has a right relationship with the trees. We need to make friends with trees, surround ourselves with them and truly live with them once again. After all, we are all made of the same stuff, because everything that exists is

240

ultimately a unity, and trees help us to see this and to make contact with "the infinite".

We can incorporate trees into our homes, building our houses around and within them in such a way that we can live in harmony. At the moment there is often a conflict which is totally unnecessary. If we can cease our fear of them, we will be able to learn from them, helping them in the way we (as moving beings) can do and allowing them to help us in the way they can. Our attitude could be more organic - to live with them rather than try to control them. Indeed, it is better to allow trees to seed naturally rather than to plant them, or as Chris Baines has rather caustically commented:

> *"Britain was a wooded country once. Woodland could return again - but not while we keep on spreading topsoil and planting trees everywhere."*[123]

It is also better if trees can be allowed to fall and die naturally and sink back into the earth rather than be grubbed up. And it was Oliver Rackham, the ecologist and landscape historian, writing about the 1987 hurricane, who pointed out that, in ecological terms, it was not the storm which was the catastrophe but the panic invasion of chain saws which followed. It is an approach which those of earlier generations and older cultures would have understood, and it is an approach we can learn from the trees themselves, if we care to listen.

Which brings me back to the essential message of this book - that trees are a parallel race of wise beings with whom we share the Earth and that they are willing to allow us access to that wisdom if we want it.

I hope that this book has shown at least part of the way forward.

References

1 anon. *A Practical Guide to Climbers, Hedges and Screens* (Bramley 1997)

2 anon. *Phallic Tree Worship - Cultus Arborum* (first published c. 1890; Bharat-Bharati 1971)

3 Aburrow, Yvonne *The Enchanted Forest* (Capall Bann 1993)

4 Aburrow, Yvonne *The Sacred Grove* (Capall Bann 1994)

5 Aikman, Anthony *Treehouses* (Hale 1988)

6 Appleton, Jay *The Experience of Landscape* (Wiley 1975)

7 Aziz, Peter in *The Sacred Tree* by Glennie Kindred (1995)

8 Bach, Edward *The Twelve Healers and Other Remedies* (C.W. Daniel 1933)

9 Baker, Richard St. Barbe *I Planted Trees* (Lutterworth 1944)

10 Bates, Brian *The Way of Wyrd* (Century 1983)

11 Bellenis, Claire *Tree Talk* in Talking Stick XIV (Spring 94)

12 Blaen, Angela *West Country Folklore No. 17 - Devon's Sacred Grove* (Toucan 1983)

13 Blamires, Heather *Rowan in Dalriada* (Samhain 1987)

14 Blamires, Steve Robert Graves' *Tree Calendar* in Talking Stick 4 (Summer 1991)

15 Blamires, Steve *Celtic Tree Mysteries* (Llewellyn 1997)

16 Bleakley, Alan *Fruits of the Moon Tree* (Gateway 1984)

17 Briagha, Ros *The Ring at Elfane* in Wood and Water Vol 2 No 31 (1990)

18 Capra, Fritjof *The Tao of Physics* (Wildwood House 1975)

19 Carbonell, Barbara M.H. *The Nymet Area* in Transactions of the Devonshire Association for the Advancement of Science, Literature and Art Vol. lxiii - 1931

20 Carr-Gomm, Philip *The Elements of The Druid Tradition* (Element Books 1991)

21 Cartwright, Julia *The Pilgrim's Way* (J.S. Virtue & Co. 1895)

22 Chapman, Craig *Sacred Groves of Britain* in Northern Earth 67 and 68 (Autumn and Winter 1996)

23 Chase, Pamela Louise and Pawlik, Jonathan *Trees for Healing* (Newcastle 1991)

24 Chetan, Anand and Brueton, Diana *The Sacred Yew* (Arkana 1994)

25 Clarke, David with Roberts, Andy *Twilight of the Celtic Gods* (Blandford 1996)

26 Clay-Egerton, Kiri - unpublished manuscript

27 Coates, Irene *Don't Panic - Paint!!* (Black Lightning Press 1984)

28 Cook, Roger *The Tree of Life* (Thames and Hudson 1974)

29 Cornish, Vaughan *Historic Thorn Trees in The British Isles* (Country Life 1941)

30 Cornish, Vaughan *The Churchyard Yew & Immortality* (Muller 1946)

31 Cresswell, Ruth Alston (compiler) *Spirit of the Trees* (Society of the Men of the Trees 1947)

32 Davies, Marion *The Magical Lore of Herbs* (Capall Bann 1994)

33 Defoe, Daniel *Robinson Crusoe* (first published 1719)

34 Devereux, Paul *Symbolic Landscapes* (Gothic Image 1992)

35 Ellis, Robin *The Woods Between the Worlds* in The Deosil Dance 34 Imbolc 1993

36 Fowles, John and Horvat, Frank *The Tree* (Aurum 1979)

37 Frazer, James G. *The Golden Bough* (Macmillan 1922)

38 Glass-Koentop, Pattalee *Year of Moons, Season of Trees* (Llewellyn 1991)

39 Goddard, Jimmy *Unusual Trees - Symbols of Leypower?* in The Ley Hunter 23 (September 1971)

40 Goudge, Elizabeth *The Herb of Grace* (Hodder and Stoughton 1948)

41 Grahame, Kenneth *The Wind in the Willows* (Methuen 1908)

42 Graves, Robert *The White Goddess* (Faber and Faber 1948)

43 Green, Marian *A Witch Alone* (Aquarian 1991)

44 Grieve, Mrs M *A Modern Herbal* (Jonathan Cape 1931)

45 Hardy, Thomas *Under the Greenwood Tree* (1872)

46 Heselton, Philip *Landscape Energy and Experience* in <u>Northern Earth Mysteries</u> 10 (Winter Solstice 1980)

47,48 Heselton, Philip *Experiencing the Subtle Geography of the Earth* in <u>Northern Earth Mysteries</u> 16 and 18 (February and July 1982)

49 Heselton, Philip; Goddard, Jimmy and Baines, Paul *Skyways and Landmarks Revisited* (Northern Earth Mysteries Group and Surrey Earth Mysteries Group 1985)

50 Heselton, Philip *Secret Places of the Goddess* (Capall Bann 1995)

51 Hodson, Geoffrey *The Kingdom of the Gods* (Theosophical Publishing House 1952)

52 Holdstock, Robert *Mythago Wood* (Gollancz 1984)

53 Jones, Evan John (with Doreen Valiente) *Witchcraft - A Tradition Renewed* (Hale 1990)

54 Kestrel *Flower Essences from Trees for Healing and Empowerment* in <u>Tree Spirit</u> (Winter Solstice 1991)

55 Kindred, Glennie *The Sacred Tree* (Glennie Kindred 1995)

56 King, Angela and Clifford, Susan (ed.) *Trees be Company* (Bristol 1989)

57 Koppana, Kati-Ma *The Finnish Gods* (Mandragora Dimensions 1990)

58 Koppana, Kati-Ma *Forest Spirits* (Mandragora Dimensions 1992)

59 Lavender, Susan and Franklin, Anna *Herb Craft - The Shamanic and Ritual Use of Herbs* (Capall Bann 1996)

60 Lee, Laurie *As I Walked Out One Midsummer Morning* (Andre Deutch 1969)

61 Lennon, Peter *Journey in the invisible world* in <u>The Guardian</u> 29 July 1997

62 Lewis, C.S. *Prince Caspian* (Geoffrey Bles 1951)

63 Lilly, Simon *Trees of Possibilities* in <u>Tree Spirit</u> (November 1996)

64 Lilly, Simon and Sue *Green Man Tree Essences* (leaflet)

65 Lorenz, Konrad *King Solomon's Ring* (Methuen 1952)

66 Lovelock, James *Gaia: A New Look at Life on Earth* (Oxford University Press 1979)

67 Mabey, Richard *Plants With A Purpose* (Collins 1977)

68 Mabey, Richard *The Common Ground* (Collins 1980)

69 Mabey, Richard *Flora Britannica* (Sinclair-Stevenson 1996)

70 Maclean, Dorothy ("Divina") *The Findhorn Garden Part 4 - Talking Trees* (The Findhorn Trust 1971)

71 Maclean, Dorothy *To Hear the Angels Sing* (Findhorn 1980)

72 McSkimming Helen *The Trees of the Celtic Alphabet* (Dalriada Celtic Heritage Society n.d.)

73 Malbert, Roger (organiser) *The Tree of Life - New Images of an Ancient Symbol* (The South Bank Centre 1989)

74 Marren, Peter *Britain's Ancient Woodland - Woodland Heritage* (David & Charles 1990)

75 Marren, Peter *The Wild Woods - A Regional Guide to Britain's Ancient Woodland* (David & Charles 1992)

76 Matthews, John *Ogam and the Sacred Woods* in <u>Caduceus</u> 35 (Spring 1997)

77 Michell, John *The Earth Spirit* (Thames and Hudson 1975)

78 Michell, John *Simulacra* (Thames and Hudson 1979)

79 Michell, John *Euphonics* (Frontier 1988)

80 Miller, Dusty *Live Wood from English Sacred Trees* (leaflet)

81 Miller, Gary *The Tree - A Return to Grace* (Lincolnshire County Council 1987)

82 Milne, A.A. *The House at Pooh Corner* (Methuen 1928)

83 Milner, J. Edward *The Tree Book* (Collins & Brown 1992)

84 Mirov, N.T. and Hasbrouck, J. *The Story of Pines* (Indiana University Press 1976)

85 Mitchell, Alan F. *The Yew in the Churchyard* in *The Tree* ed. Peter Wood (David & Charles 1990)

86 Moore, Jeremy *After the Wildwood - An Exploration of People and Trees* (Wrexham Library Arts Centre 1990)

87 Morton, Andrew *The Trees of Shropshire* (Airlife 1986)

88 Murray, Liz and Colin *The Celtic Tree Oracle* (Rider 1988)

89 Nuttall, G. Clarke *Trees and How They Grow* (Cassell 1913)

90 Pakenham, Thomas *Meetings with Remarkable Trees* (Weidenfeld & Nicolson 1996)

91 Paterson, Jacqueline Memory *Tree Wisdom* (Thorsons 1996)

92 Pennick, Nigel *Earth Harmony* (Century 1987; revised second edition, Capall Bann 1997)

93 Phillips, Guy Ragland *Brigantia* (Routledge & Kegan Paul 1976)

94 Philpot, J.H. *The Sacred Tree or The Tree in Religion and Myth* (first published 1897; Llanerch 1994)

95 Rackham, Oliver *Trees and Woodland in the British Landscape* (Dent 1976)

96 Ransome, Arthur *Swallows and Amazons* (Jonathan Cape 1930)

97 Ransome, Arthur *Swallowdale* (Jonathan Cape 1931)

98 Ransome, Arthur *Pigeon Post* (Jonathan Cape 1936)

99 Raven, Morgan *Communicating with Nature Spirits* in <u>The Unicorn</u> 4

100 Richardson, Brian - personal communication to author

101 Rider, Carl *Your Psychic Power* (Piatkus 1988)

102 Sempers, Chris *The Celtic Tree* Calendar (Raven 1993)

103 Sheldrake, Rupert *A New Science of Life* (Blond & Briggs 1981)

104 Sheldrake, Rupert *The Rebirth of Nature* (Century 1990)

105 Stone, Alby *A Splendid Pillar* (Heart of Albion 1992)

106 Tansley, A.G. *The British Islands and their Vegetation* (Cambridge University Press 1939)

107 Taplin, Kim *Tongues in Trees* (Green Books 1989)

108 Titterington, Chris *The Legible Tree - The Pictorial Language of Trees in British Landscape Painting* in Gary Miller, *The Tree - A Return to Grace* (Lincolnshire County Council 1987)

109 Trevelyan, George *The Active Eye in Architecture* (Wrekin Trust 1977)

110 Valiente, Doreen *An ABC of Witchcraft Past & Present* (Hale 1973)

111 Valiente, Doreen *Witchcraft for Tomorrow* (Hale 1978)

112 Valiente, Doreen *The Rebirth of Witchcraft* (Hale 1989)

113 Vickery, Roy *Oxford Dictionary of Plant Lore* (Oxford University Press 1995)

114 "W.G." *A Useful Tree-spell* in <u>Pentagram</u> 3 (March 1965)

115 Watkins, Alfred *The Old Straight Track* (Methuen 1925)

116 Wedd, Tony *Skyways and Landmarks* (STAR Fellowship 1961)

117 Wedd, Tony *The Way, The Truth and The Light* in <u>The Ley Hunter</u> 3 (January 1970)

118 Wedd, Tony *Plenty without Pyramids* (unpublished manuscript)

119 Whitlock, Ralph *The Oak* (Allen and Unwin 1985)

120 Whone, Herbert *Touch Wood - A Journey Among Trees* (Smith Settle 1990)

121 Wilkinson, Gerald *Trees in the Wild* (Book Club Associates 1975)

122 Wilks, J.H. *Trees of the British Isles in History & Legend* (Muller 1972)

123 Wood, Peter (ed.) *The Tree* (David & Charles 1990)

Further Reading

One of the main reasons which led me to write this book was that there did not seem to be anything which adequately covered the field which I wanted to cover.

However, I have drawn from a variety of sources, as one look at the 'References' section will confirm, and some of these have been consistently helpful.

Two classic texts that have to be included are Sir James Frazer's *The Golden Bough* and Robert Graves' *The White Goddess*. Trees are really the central theme running through both books and there is a wealth of traditional custom, folklore and legend within their pages.

When we look at individual species, pride of place must go to *Tree Wisdom* by Jacqueline Memory Paterson. There is a long chapter on each of 17 different species, going into the folklore, remedies and essential character in a way which is both very thorough and inspirational.

Also very good on the underlying character of each species are *The Trees of the Celtic Alphabet* by Helen McSkimming and *The Sacred Tree* by Glennie Kindred. Both are only booklets but they get to the heart of things much better than many other larger volumes.

As I have already mentioned, poetry about trees is a common theme, and there are at least three good anthologies, including *Touch Wood* by Herbert Whone (which includes some remarkable photographs and which I have mentioned in Chapter 4), *Spirit of the Trees* by Ruth Alston Cresswell and

Trees be Company by Angela King and Sue Clifford. All have a wonderful selection of poems, which move and inspire.

A good introduction to some of the wealth of literature on the subject is Kim Taplin's *Tongues in Trees*, which is subtitled '*Studies in Literature and Ecology*'.

Books on individual species of tree are rare, but I must include the excellent book by Anand Chetan and Diana Brueton entitled *The Sacred Yew - Rediscovering the ancient Tree of Life through the work of Allen Meredith*.

Pattalee Glass-Koentop's *Year of Moons, Season of Trees*, Pamela Louise Chase and Jonathan Pawlik's *Trees for Healing*, Steve Blamires' *Celtic Tree Mysteries* and John Fowles and Frank Horvat's *The Tree* have also been major sources of inspiration.

I hope very much that Kiri Clay-Egerton's manuscript will be published before too long, as it has certainly been a continuous inspiration to me.

Whilst it was published as long ago as 1913, and thus long out of print, G. Clarke Nuttall's *Trees and How they Grow* has been very revealing of the manifestation of the energies within each species.

And the writings of Vaughan Cornish, Robin Ellis, Kati-Ma Koppana, Susan Lavender & Anna Franklin, Richard Mabey, Peter Marren, John Michell and Doreen Valiente have all contributed greatly to my understanding of our relationship to trees.

Index

blackthorn, 116-119, 214, 220-221
Blaen, Angela, 206, 242
Blamires, Heather, 76, 242
Blamires, Steve, 86, 90-91, 242, 249
Bleakley, Alan, 207, 235, 242
blossom, 117-118, 126-127, 159, 161
bodhi tree, 45, 71
bonfires, 25, 233
Boscobel, 18
boundaries, 10, 13, 53, 113-114, 200, 213
Boutros-Ghali, Boutros, 3
bowers, 20
box, 208, 227, 236
brainwaves, 77
brambles, 98
Briagha, Ros, 213, 242
broomsticks, 105, 114
Brown, Capability, 203
Brueton, Diana, 47, 243, 249
Buddha, 45, 56, 61, 71
Buddhism, 56

Caesar, 105
Caledonian Forest, 46
calendars, 100, 105, 139, 159, 161-165, 208, 214, 242, 246
Capra, Fritjof, 242
Carr-Gomm, Philip, 163-165, 242
Cartwright, Julia, 201, 243
carvings, 65
Casson, Hugh, 62
caves, 17
Cawston, Norfolk, 39

celebrations, 17, 52, 139, 240
chakras, 31, 33, 93
charcoal-burners, 23
Charlemagne, 59
Charles II, 18
Chase, Pamela Louise, 56, 86, 90, 243, 249
Chetan, Anand, 47, 243, 249
Chiddingstone, Kent, 37, 195
Chiltern Hills, 105
China, 52
Christianity, 15, 49, 52, 56, 66, 124, 139, 155, 173, 191, 211-212
churches, 15, 19-20, 50, 66, 139, 199-201, 206, 208, 210-212, 234
churchyards, 52, 155, 208, 210-211
circles, 18, 20, 82, 141, 180, 188, 193, 207, 210, 213-214, 218-221, 232
clairvoyance, 122
Clarke, David 190, 243
Clay-Egerton, Kiri, 47, 83, 167, 181, 189, 243, 249
Clifford, Sue, 68, 244
climbing, 6, 18-20, 53, 197
clumps, 7, 37, 39, 195, 197-200, 202, 207-208, 211, 234
Coates, Irene, 62-63, 243
Cole's Tump, 198-199
Collis, John Stewart, 13
concealment, 68, 187
Conchobar, 155
confusion, 187

family trees, 57
Farndon, 11
felling, 21, 210
fertility, 49, 55-56, 97, 110,
    114-115, 126-127
festivity, 139
Findhorn, 45, 61, 245
Finland, 179-180, 244
fire, 23-25, 86-87, 102-103,
    137, 214, 222
Fletcher, Fred, 7
flowers, 55, 59, 91, 117, 121,
    126, 129-130, 134, 207,
    221, 229, 236, 238
Fly agaric, 114
folklore, 1, 26, 40-41, 48-51,
    55, 60, 87, 96-98, 102, 141,
    163, 242, 248
Fowles, John, 51, 65, 88, 167,
    171, 187, 205, 218, 240,
    243, 249
Franklin, Anna, 109, 113,
    118, 141, 244, 249
Frazer, James, 52-54, 56, 243,
    248
Frost, Robert, 18,
fruits, 21, 26, 59, 73, 117,
    121, 130, 165, 221, 229,
    237, 242

Gaia, 33, 244
gardens, 46
garlands, 221, 223
gateways, 45, 47, 180, 192,
    242
Germany, 56
Gill's Lap, 197, 199

Glass-Koentop, Pattalee, 42,
    52, 229, 243, 249
Glastonbury, 11
Gloucestershire, 47
Goddard, Jimmy, 37, 54, 243-
    244
goddesses, 50
gods, 50, 53, 59, 66, 212, 218,
    243-244
gorse, 98, 163, 186, 193
Gospel Oak, 139
Goudge, Elizabeth, 12, 243
Grahame, Kenneth, 67, 243
Graves, Robert, 52, 69, 105,
    114, 129, 132, 155, 162-
    164, 235, 242-243, 248
Great Yews, 210
Greece, 33, 45, 51, 54, 59,
    141, 179, 230
Green Man, 18, 51, 66, 212,
    238, 244
greenwood, 12, 17, 66-67,
    170, 222, 234, 243
grief, 149, 151
groves, 5, 45, 54, 56-57, 105,
    107, 141, 153, 156, 179,
    185, 188, 198, 205-208,
    210-214, 230-231, 233, 235,
    238, 242-243

Hag, 118, 122
hamadryads, 179
Hardy, Thomas 17, 67, 115,
    141, 169, 234, 243
Hathor, 52
hawthorn, 6, 18, 35, 95, 99,
    117, 119, 121, 124-127,
    162, 165, 214, 220-221, 236

A selection of other Capall Bann titles. Free catalogue available.

Secret Places of the Goddess by Philip Heselton

This book is a practical and evocative encouragement to seek the Earth Spirit in those special places where it dwells, embracing a wide definition of Paganism to include all those inner yearnings towards a closer contact with the land. It will appeal to all who are drawn to visit such natural and archetypal locations in the landscape as tree groves, sacred springs, special rock outcrops, the seashore and the Wild Wood. All these are Secret Places of the Goddess. The author shows why certain locations have been considered numinous and magical and how we can each go about finding these special places in the landscape. He provides a vision of the variety of ways in which we might respond to the spirit present at such sites and thereby enter into a closer relationship with the Old Ones.
ISBN 1898307 40 7   £10.95

Mirrors of Magic - Evoking the Spirit of the Dewponds by Philip Heselton

The image of the pond lies deep within our psyche. The abundant legend and folklore which surrounds ponds and pools, interpreted rightly, reveals the relationship which country people still had with the spirit of the landscape within living memory. This book shows that these "mirrors of magic" are locations where consciousness can be changed to experience the earth spirit and to perform acts of divination and magic. It also explores the powerful and recurring image of the Moon reflected in the still water of the pool and reveals how this has traditionally been used in magical ritual.
ISBN 1898307 84 9   £9.95

Herb Craft - A Guide to the Shamanic and Ritual Use of Herbs
by Susan Lavender and Anna Franklin

This herbal moves beyond the folklore associated with herbs and examines their true magical nature. It examines how power plants can be employed for the transformation of Self and consciousness, according to the teachings of Native Pagan Tradition. Detailed descriptions of herbs are included, together with a guide to cultivating them for magical purposes, their traditional uses, explanations of their lore, the art of the herb simpler, (healer) and traditional recipes. Correspondences are also included- animal totems, associated tools, deities, planets, elements and festivals. The herbs are set out in an easy to use alphabetical form and are followed by appendices designed to help each individual with their own personal development.
ISBN 1898307 57 1   £19.95   600 pages

The Enchanted Forest - The Magical Lore of Trees
by Yvonne Aburrow

Fascinating & truly unique - a comprehensive guide to the magical, medicinal & craft uses, mythology, folklore, symbolism & weatherlore of trees. There are chapters on trees in myth & legend, tree spirits, trees in ritual magic, trees & alphabets (runes & Ogham) & weather lore. These chapters are followed by a comprehensive 'herbal index' with in-depth coverage of individual trees from acacia to aspen, wayfaring tree to willow. Profusely illustrated.
ISBN 1898307 083   £10.95

A selection of other Capall Bann titles. Free catalogue available.

Practical Spirituality by Steve Hounsome

Many people today struggle with attempting to blend a spiritual life with the demands of work, home and family. For many, the rampant commercialism, exploitation and consequent destruction of the modern 'developed' world is in direct conflict with the sacred ideals held so dear by those who seek to live the way of the spirit. This book addresses this problem, offering a means whereby the dedicated, serious practitioner can learn to live a practical, spiritual life, with what is sacred to them at its heart and as its focus. This is achieved by close association with the natural world, the wheel of nature round its annual cycle and the Elements that constitute its life. There are many practical exercises included to help you find your way. Indeed we may well find that it is by living this way that society is changed, since all effective change must come from within. ISBN 186163 015 8 £10.95

Wildlife Gardening by Ron Wilson

It's a fact that most people can't plan their garden from 'scratch', but a few 'modifications' and additions could enhance its value for wildlife. That is what this book is all about. It offers practical advice and ideas for improvements and where possible suggests the inclusion of 'extra' features. Plants, foods and features are all described in plain English. The trouble with some wildlife gardening books is that you have to be an 'expert', whatever 'expert' means, everything in this book is explained in straightforward terms to enable anyone to help their local wildlife.
ISBN 1 86163 011 5   £10.95

The Sacred Grove - The Mysteries of the Forest by Yvonne Aburrow

The veneration of trees was a major theme in the paganism of the Romans, Greeks, Celtic & Germanic peoples. Many of their rites took place in sacred groves & much of their symbolism involved the cosmic tree; its branches supported the heavens, its trunk was the centre of the earth & its roots penetrated the underworld. This book explains the various mysteries of the tree & how these can be incorporated into modern paganism. This gives a new perspective on the cycle of seasonal festivals.
ISBN   1898307 12 1   £10.95

The Healing Book by Chris Thomas & Diane Baker

This book is for those who wish to heal, starting at the beginning of the healing process with simple, easily followed exercises which can begin to unlock the healing potential which is inherent in all of us. Nobody needs to feel left out of these abilities. We are all healers, all that we need to do is to stop telling ourselves that we are not. Whatever level of experience you have of healing, this book explains in simple uncomplicated language that does not use mysticism or any form of ritual, how to understand the "Chakras" and the way in which our daily lives influences them, to relate medical conditions to the chakras and to learn methods which will bring the chakras back into balance, both for yourself and for others. These methods apply equally to humans and to animals. If you do not have any experience of giving healing, but would like to learn, this book can set you on that path. If you already work as a healer, in whatever capacity, and would like to explore your greater potential, this book is also for you.
ISBN 186163 053 0   £8.95

FREE DETAILED CATALOGUE

A detailed illustrated catalogue is available on request, SAE or International Postal Coupon appreciated. **Titles can be ordered direct from Capall Bann, post free in the UK** (cheque or PO with order) or from good bookshops and specialist outlets. Titles currently available include:

Animals, Mind Body Spirit & Folklore
Angels and Goddesses - Celtic Christianity & Paganism by Michael Howard
Arthur - The Legend Unveiled by C Johnson & E Lung
Auguries and Omens - The Magical Lore of Birds by Yvonne Aburrow
Book of the Veil The by Peter Paddon
Caer Sidhe - Celtic Astrology and Astronomy by Michael Bayley
Call of the Horned Piper by Nigel Jackson
Cats' Company by Ann Walker
Celtic Lore & Druidic Ritual by Rhiannon Ryall
Compleat Vampyre - The Vampyre Shaman: Werewolves & Witchery by Nigel Jackson
Crystal Clear - A Guide to Quartz Crystal by Jennifer Dent
Earth Dance - A Year of Pagan Rituals by Jan Brodie
Earth Harmony - Places of Power, Holiness and Healing by Nigel Pennick
Earth Magic by Margaret McArthur
Enchanted Forest - The Magical Lore of Trees by Yvonne Aburrow
Familiars - Animal Powers of Britain by Anna Franklin
Healing Homes by Jennifer Dent
Herbcraft - Shamanic & Ritual Use of Herbs by Susan Lavender & Anna Franklin
In Search of Herne the Hunter by Eric Fitch
Magical Incenses and Perfumes by Jan Brodie
Magical Lore of Cats by Marion Davies
Magical Lore of Herbs by Marion Davies
Masks of Misrule - The Horned God & His Cult in Europe by Nigel Jackson
Mysteries of the Runes by Michael Howard
Patchwork of Magic by Julia Day
Psychic Self Defence - Real Solutions by Jan Brodie
Runic Astrology by Nigel Pennick
Sacred Animals by Gordon MacLellan
Sacred Grove - The Mysteries of the Forest by Yvonne Aburrow
Sacred Geometry by Nigel Pennick
Sacred Lore of Horses The by Marion Davies
Sacred Ring - Pagan Origins British Folk Festivals & Customs by Michael Howard
Seasonal Magic - Diary of a Village Witch by Paddy Slade
Secret Places of the Goddess by Philip Heselton
Talking to the Earth by Gordon Maclellan
Taming the Wolf - Full Moon Meditations by Steve Hounsome
The Goddess Year by Nigel Pennick & Helen Field
West Country Wicca by Rhiannon Ryall

Capall Bann is owned and run by people actively involved in many of the areas in which we publish. Our list is expanding rapidly so do contact us for details on the latest releases.

Capall Bann Publishing, Freshfields, Chieveley, Berks, RG20 8TF